This book, *Leadership & Me*, is considered a must read for every current and aspiring CEO.
Philip through insightful reflection raises significant issues about leadership and management from within the realities of his life and work experience. Issues, such as the importance of building Brand Recognition, Strategic Thinking, Team Leadership, Personal and Workplace Relationships, the dangers of well-intentioned, but not helpful, micromanagement and operational detail being advocated by outsiders.
Organisational Change is difficult and involves building strong, trusted relationships based on shared values, organisational purpose and personal beliefs. Philip shares his struggles and successes, both in leadership and personal, with insightful comments and courageous honesty.

Ian Allsop, BA, BD, MBA, PhD—Past Senior Fellow, Melbourne Business School, Past Federal Secretary Churches of Christ in Australia

I finished Philip's book *Leadership & Me* with a deep sense of gratitude. Grateful for the wisdom that lay within the pages, and grateful for the albeit brief time that I was able to work with Philip and learn some of these lessons first hand. Finally, I am grateful that there are people such as Philip in the world, striving to make it better and leaving those that follow a path and now a map.

David McNamara—CEO, Foodbank Victoria

I accompanied Philip Hunt, a famous musician and a film crew to Mozambique for a *40 Hour Famine* filmshoot way back when. As we traversed this extremely dangerous country during a 10 year civil war, I remember asking Philip how I could have his job. Simple, he replied, just do a Master's in International Development or an MBA and you will be on your way. Reading *Leadership & Me*, one could almost believe his career trajectory from glorified bank clerk to CEO of World Vision was as simple as that. Philip's matter-of-fact, self-reflective account of leadership lessons learned as he career-hopped into a communications role at World Vision Australia, culminating in the internal CEO appointment, give insights into culture building, vision setting and office politics. He is honest about his failures and his inability to read the tea leaves (the CEO/chairperson relationship is paramount to success). The book intersperses stories of family with job and faith, reminding us that home life leaks into work and *vice versa*. Philip has made significant contributions to the nonprofit sector, not just through World Vision Australia, but also World Vision International, Deakin University and the Foodbank. Don't be deceived by his accessible, personable writing style. There are life lessons on almost every page!

Penny Mulvey—Chief Communications Officer, Bible Society Australia

Philip Hunt makes a powerful case that inspired effective leadership is essential for transformative work with children and families in global poverty. *Leadership & Me* is his compelling story of asking tough questions and looking for answers in his 25 years as a leader in World Vision Australia and World Vision Hong Kong. All of this is told with great storytelling, Philip's faith and his wry humour.
    ***Dave Toycen**—Retired CEO, World Vision Canada*

In his book *Leadership & Me*, Philip tells his story of challenges faced in leadership roles. While the dominant context relates to World Vision in Australia, it also includes his international leadership roles with World Vision in Hong Kong, Singapore, the Middle East, and Eastern Europe and other Australian organisations (after World Vision).
Through his life experiences, intellectual rigour and with the encouragement of mentors, Philip sought to bring about change. Always interested in the "what" and "why", he embraced the theme of change. Sometimes it was a matter of creating the momentum for change. At other times it was responding to opportunities.
His book identifies themes relating to managing stakeholder expectations, understanding diverse agendas and contrary voices, the process and pace of change. It provides an insight into how his God given gifts were developed and refined over time. A recommended read for anyone engaged in leading change, especially within the social sector.
    ***John Rose**—World Vision Australia & World Vision International 1978—2005*

Leadership & Me

Wisdom & Life Lessons of a World Vision Australia CEO

Philip Hunt

Cardinia Ranges Publishing House
Beaconsfield, Victoria 3807, Australia
cardiniaranges.com
info@cardiniaranges.com

Leadership & Me: Wisdom & Life Lessons of a World Vision Australia CEO
Copyright ©2021 by Philip Hunt
First published 2021

All rights reserved. Apart from any fair dealing for the purpose of private study, research, criticism or review, as permitted under the Copyright Act, no part may be reproduced by any process without written permission. Inquiries should be addressed to the publisher.

Cardinia Ranges Publishing House exists with the mission of inspiring people to fulfill their God-given potential.

ISBN: 978-1-922537-02-7 (print edition)
ISBN: 978-1-922537-03-4 (EPUB edition)
ISBN: 978-1-922537-04-1 (Mobi & Kindle edition)

 A catalogue record for this book is available from the National Library of Australi

Cover & interior book design: Jozua van Otterloo
Cover photographs: Aidan Truscott

Contents

Foreword	ix
Book 1–Following	**1**
1 The End Of A Dream	3
2 Often Wrong: Never in Doubt	5
3 How Did I Do It?	7
4 We Learn From Those We Copy	9
5 It's Not All About Me	13
6 Honor The System And It Will Work For You	17
7 Systems Work, If You've Made The Right Assumptions	21
8 Radio Daze	27
9 Babyhood Changes You For Good	31

Book 2–Just Managing — 35
10 Your Work Is A Serious Business — 37
11 Begin With A Vision — 41
12 Work With Experts–Listen And Learn — 47
13 Manage People–Avoid Power — 53
14 The Best For God's Work–Stay Grounded — 57

Book 3–Go East Young Man — 63
15 Go To The People, Live With Them, Learn From Them — 65
16 Child Sponsorship Needed Fixing — 75
17 Oriental And Lifestyle Questions — 79
18 Make Mistakes–Learn From Them — 85

Book 4–Displaced At Home — 89
19 Not That Job, This Job–Maybe I Should Quit — 91
20 Stress Can Make You Sick — 95
21 Primal Scream Therapy — 99
22 When Life Serves Up Lemons, Make Lemonade — 103
23 Challenge The Taken-for-granted Assumptions — 107
24 Leaders, I've Had A Few — 111
25 Learn From Those Who Have Walked The Talk — 115
26 When Change Is Too Slow, Change Things Slowly — 119
27 Values And Beliefs Matter — 127
28 Be A Drover, Not A Driver — 131

Book 5–Getting The Big Picture — 135
29 When The Mission Statement Is Wrong, Change It — 137
30 Where You Stand Depends On Where You Sit — 141
31 Grab Opportunity Without A Fanfare — 147
32 All Change At The Top — 153
33 An Empty Chair Is An Invitation — 157

Contents

Book 6 – Got The Gig, Now What? — 165
34 Clean The Curtains, Share Out The Real Work — 167
35 Listen To The Stories You Tell — 173
36 Find A Vision That Empowers Everyone — 179
37 Inch By Inch Anything's A Cinch — 185
38 Only Collaborate Where You Don't Compete — 193
39 Make Money Decisions That Work — 199
40 Trickle Down Theory Of Imparting The Vision — 205
41 Integrity Is The Bedrock Of Reputation — 209

Book 7 – The Challenge Of Challenging The Status Quo — 217
42 Give Your Ideas Away, Trust People — 219
43 Future Surprises, Sometimes You Don't See Them Coming — 223
44 Success Can Hide Tomorrow's Problems — 225
45 If You're Dissatisfied, Don't Just Sit There, Do Something — 229
46 Listen To The Next Generation. It's Their Future, Not Yours — 233
47 Transfer Or Transform Is The Core Issue — 235
48 Don't Lose The Wonder — 239
49 Board Development Is A Continuous And Intensive Process — 241
50 Search The Future, Recognise What You Know — 247
51 Give Accountability To People, Not Teams — 249

Book 8 – The Edges Fray — 253
52 It's Going Well, But... — 255
53 Liminal Work Towards A New Organisation — 259
54 Chickens Do Come Home To Roost — 263
55 Talk To Peers–You Are Not On This Journey Alone — 267
56 Cut Off At The Pass — 269
57 The End Of One Story — 273
58 Drifting — 279
59 Afterword — 289

About The Author — 293

Foreword

by Tim Costello

This is the story of a man who happens to be extraordinarily talented. His story is beguiling in his ordinariness, but this ordinariness envelopes his huge talent which leads him to becoming the leader of Australia's largest charity, World Vision. And without him ever saying it (but I can) it became Australia's largest charity in large measure because of the spirituality, vision and leadership of this one man–*Philip Hunt*.

For those wanting to understand how an obscure American Christian charity could set up office in Little Collins Street, Melbourne, in 1966 with a typewriter and volunteers licking stamps, to now operating in over 60 countries and $500 million of annual income today? The answer in a large part was that Philip became the communications or marketing director in the years of its phenomenal growth. Then, after years of faithful work, he was recognised by becoming its CEO for nine years. And this journey all started on the copywriter's desk.

Philip charts his early life in rural Queensland, his parents and church and the powerful influence of Dr Lew Born who mentored him and so many other outstanding leaders. Philip relates his early jobs working on night shift radio stations and a chance invitation to work at World Vision in 1976. At this time, World Vision was still microscopically small and certainly not a household name.

To give the reader some perspective: the mother ship US World Vision, which has been running for over 70 years, is still today unknown to most Americans. In Australia, it is not just a household name but many of today's generation of politicians will tell you that when they did the *40 Hour Famine* as high school students their eyes were opened to privilege, power and powerlessness and for many it seeded their journey into public life. The *40 Hour Famine* was a rite of passage for hundreds of thousands of Australian students—a much healthier rite of passage than *schoolies* week. And who was effectively the pioneer of the *40 Hour Famine*? Philip Hunt and his then boss, David Longe.

But success was not linear and in this story the challenges and bumps are honestly discussed. The making of Philip as a leader to keep the World Vision mob (staff) heading in the right direction was tough. His struggle to model the values and behave consistently as a leader is discussed with refreshing candour. And his struggles to move the vision from a transactional fundraising office to a transforming relationship that empowers both donors and the poor in the field, is all part of Philip's vision and legacy.

His life with World Vision later took him and his family to open the World Vision office in Hong Kong (also a fabulously successful office) and later to Vienna to look after 'easy' places to manage like the Middle East. Throughout all this, Philip's humour and humility shines through.

World Vision is known for its bright orange logo and is called in the development field "the big Orange". In writing this book, Philip has been vulnerable and opened the orange Kimino that clothes World Vision and invited us to take a peep. I, for one, am deeply grateful as though serving as a successor to Philip as CEO, I had never really understood the complete World Vision journey. Reading this story gave me pride that I was also able to be part of this remarkable story—and a richer awareness of the impact others have had in the formation of the values, structures and reputation I tended to take as granted.

This is an insightful Australian story—grounded, humble, honest and perceptive. It is a journey of self-insight with lashings of self-deprecation by a man I am honoured to call an associate and a friend.

Tim Costello AO
CEO World Vision Australia 2004-2016

Book 1

Following

I

The End Of A Dream

Don't quote me, but this is how I remember it.

There was a Board Meeting. It was a closed-door meeting. I hated closed-door meetings. I'd asked the architects, who'd designed the World Vision Australia office in Burwood East, to install glass walls in every meeting room.

David Jenkin was chair of the Board... at the start of the meeting, anyway. David had appointed me as CEO in 1988, plucking me from colleagues, most of whom I had worked with for over a decade.

Did David wise me up about resigning the chair? I can't remember. Perhaps I should have seen it coming.

David's life was busy and surrounded by a whirl of challenges: A wife in need of a kidney (David supplied one of his). A full-time career at the head of the Melbourne Central Project after a stellar career with Myer as a department-store retailer. He had recently become Chair of the international Board of World Vision. David had enough to go on with. It was only reasonable that he would shed one of his local roles. No-one would begrudge him that. I didn't. *But the earth shifted.*

How did it come to this? A fresh chair elected. An instant showdown. A brick of despair in my gut. Bewilderment that it was all my fault. A decade and a half of learning, trying, improving had reached a moment when revolutionary organisational change might position World Vision Australia for the 21st century. This was set aside. A pause.

I felt abandoned and suddenly unsupported. And worse, I felt we were betraying the nearly four hundred colleagues who worked with me every day to make World Vision Australia not merely a household name, but such a special example of God's justice and love.

That's a short story. And a longer one.

The short story—of my failed attempt to prepare an international aid agency for the 21st century—can be told quickly. There's not much useful to learn from it apart from my own follies and misreading of the tea leaves.

The longer story—how someone came to work asking, "How can I make things better?"—may contain something more useful.

If you just want the short story, skip to the last chapters. Maybe some of you will come back here.

* * *

2

Often Wrong: Never In Doubt

All my life, the strangest thing keeps happening.

I enter a group of four people standing together in the after-church coffee confusion. They make space. We are now five. Their conversation continues without interruption. I pick up the thread of the topic and listen.

Before long, and often before I have opened my mouth except to sip my coffee, I observe that my companions address their contributions to me. Perhaps they want to draw me into the conversation. They are including me. Perhaps they want some response from me. They value my opinion. All this is a natural group dynamic.

Yet, there is something else at play, because this will often happen in a formal meeting in which someone else is chairing. I may take care to occupy a seat of least authority. I sit at the side of the table, far away from the chairperson at the head place. The rules ought to be clear.

Address the chair, *not me*. Yet, speakers will sometimes direct their comments towards me. Often, to me *alone*.

I am embarrassed. My body language shifts. I break eye contact with the speaker. I look down at my notes. The speaker may sense the polite rebuke and address the chair or the assembly. I look up. The gaze returns toward me...

This is not something I am seeking. I feel for others in the meeting. I worry they think it is my deliberate ploy; that I am an attention seeker. When it is my turn to speak, I consciously show respect for the chair and include the group in my gaze.

I used to wonder why this happens. I may have no authority in this group. I am not smarter, older or better looking than the others. Look around. What's going on?

Judy, my life partner, wife, mother of my children and believer-in-me says, "It's your confidence. It's what attracted me to you." Apparently not my fine looks then.

It seems I exude confidence. Really? Why don't I feel more confident?

"It's a Pegler thing," said my Aunty Lois, my father's younger sister. Lois Hunt was a teacher, deputy-principal and a capable woman who adored her nieces and nephews, perhaps as surrogates for not having her own kids.

Lois Hunt was the daughter of Nellie Pegler, our Gran. She, in turn, was the daughter of Walter Pegler, our great-grandfather in whose house we lived in Parramatta, west of Sydney.

"The Peglers are all like this," Aunty Lois claimed. "Confident. Often wrong, but never in doubt. It's a burden we have to bear."

However, *it is also a gift*.

* * *

3

How Did I Do It?

"I have to admit, I don't understand how Philip works." This is not what I expected Dean Hirsch, the President of World Vision International and my boss, to say at my farewell after 24 years with World Vision.

He continued, "I don't understand how Philip works, but whatever, he gets things done. *He's good.*"

A little over twelve years earlier, a previous boss of mine had said something similar. Not about me. About himself.

Harold Henderson was my first boss in World Vision Australia. I had enjoyed two periods under his leadership when, in 1989, Harold resigned to take up a position with World Vision International. On a December evening, the Australian staff and their families traipsed to a reception centre in Canterbury, Melbourne to say farewell. It was a summer evening, made warmer by appreciative and worthy words.

Many expressed a lot of love for Harold, but I recall only Harold's response. And my surprise.

Harold admitted, in a typically self-deprecating way, that all the success that World Vision Australia had enjoyed during the decade-and-a-half of his leadership, was a mystery to him. He may not have exactly said, "I don't know how we did it," but that was the sense of it. It surprised me. I thought I knew exactly how "we did it". It was because of how Harold himself "did it."

Even at that point, halfway through my working life, I saw Harold had a method that worked. If I had been in tune with the moment, I should have said something like this.

"Harold, here's how you did it.

"First, you have an eye for talent. You employed good people. Sometimes you even would put someone on when you didn't really have a job for them. You just had a hunch their gifts would be useful. Some of us wondered about this, but you were usually right.

"Second, you gave people a sense of purpose. We picked it up from you. You didn't deliver it like a doctrine, or even a grandiose key objective. Rather, it emerged in conversation and discussion. You gave it away. We owned it.

"Third, you gave us freedom. The level of trust I experienced was beyond generous. We responded with a determination to never let you down. We would not betray your belief in us.

"Fourth, you kept the herd generally heading west. You encouraged us to grow, to fix things that were wrong, to invent, to work with the willing, to encourage the unwilling on to their careers elsewhere, to maintain the momentum."

I wish I had said all that. That is what I was learning. Over the next two decades I took these principles into leadership roles in World Vision Australia (as Harold's successor), to an international role in the Middle East and Eastern Europe, into my consulting business, into two medium term turnaround tasks at a university student union and a food recovery organisation, into a busy retirement and my second multi-million dollar building project, and finally to a general management role in a city church.

This is the story of how that panned out.

* * *

4

We Learn From Those We Copy

We learn by copying those we admire. Parents. My draughtsman Dad became a business executive. John Morris Hunt was well organised, thoughtful and capable. Without thinking or recognising it, I wanted to be just like him. Growing up is like that. We live in blissful unawareness of how our minds are being shaped.

So, I realise now that parents, extended family members, teachers, leaders in the church, all provided models of leadership that shaped me. In my teen years, I became a church organist. Is it any surprise that I saw my mother and an uncle in that role as a child? I watched my father drive his Renaults, Humber and the big Sunday School bus. No surprise I should grow up interested in cars.

I sat in classes under teachers of varying capabilities. Some of them impressed me without my realising it. Some I must have admired and copied (Mr Thorpe in Third Class comes to mind). A few influenced me as not to be emulated.

One influential leader of young people in the Queensland Methodist Church was Dr Lew Born. Or just Doc to most of us.

During the Queensland Spring school holidays, Doc organised Gold Coast camps that attracted over a thousand secondary school kids. Here was boot camp for managers and leaders.

So much to learn. An administration system that lined up applications with payments. An organisational hierarchy that placed roles and responsibility in logical order. I was a camper. Next year I was responsible for a "team" of campers as a "team leader." Another year, a "staffer" responsible for an aspect of the daily program. Above it all, inspiring and correcting, was Lew Born. Teaching us about leading. And we sponged it all up.

Today, all over Australia and the world, I see men and women who got their grounding in organisational life and practice under the influence of Lew Born and his ilk.

Doc also directed a monthly rally of Methodist Youth. The model borrowed from the Secondary School Camp experience. Volunteers. Clearly defined roles. High expectations. Doc insisted on high production values. Membership of the team meant commitment.

"First Saturday Night say 'Sorry'" meant blocking out the first Saturday of every month. We fully rehearsed during the afternoon.

"No gaps" became a mantra for producing a tight, slick program. You knew when to come on, which microphone to stand at (and how close), never to blow into a mike, and the sound tech knew to have the mike ON the moment you inhaled.

Leading the music, the more capable Steve Nisbet played the Wurlitzer organ. I played piano to accompany. I enjoyed living in the penumbra. Not in the spotlight; not in the dark.

Doc always wanted to improve the program, to enhance the experience, to want them coming back for more. He was training tomorrow's presenters, technicians, producers, directors, managers and more. And I noticed that Doc got a lot of things done, even though he wasn't doing much of the actual doing.

Throughout life there have been other mentors. Sometimes it has just been a word at the right time. Bruce Redpath was CEO of Mayne Nickless when we sat together in a bus. During the 30-minute ride, one sentence took root.

"Chief Executives are there to change things. If you're not changing things, what are you there for?"

I would see plenty of leaders content with the status quo. I would not be one of them.

Dr Ted Engstrom was already a legend in World Vision when I joined in 1976. Known unofficially as the *Man Who Saved World Vision* in the 1960s, he believed in and taught MBO: Management By Objectives. He was a structured and disciplined leader, yet two other things impressed me more.

First, once I came within his sightline, he would note a move in my career path with a personal message of encouragement. Amazing how encouraging it is to be noticed.

Second, Ted's many mantras included "If people think right, they'll do right." He had an after-dinner talk based on the Rotary "Four Way Test". I learned from this brilliant MBO lecturer that culture, values and ethics matter.

The practice of these insights would not always put me in favour. One member of my World Vision Australia Board informed the meeting: "We appear to have a staff who do not think of their chief executive as their boss, but as their friend." I was momentarily glad he'd noticed, until I realised he did not mean it kindly.

I shall always treasure Milton Morris's description of me as "like a clock in a thunderstorm: ticking steadily on."

But all this is for later.

Meanwhile, I went to *the Village*.

* * *

5

It's Not All About Me

In the Sixties, Schoolies had not been invented, but that did not deter thousands of teenagers from rocking up to the Gold Coast every summer. Lazy days at the beach segued into wild nights.

For some years, Methodist youth had attempted to channel some of that wildness in safer ways. A few hundred young people organised discos in the church halls of Surfers Paradise, Burleigh Heads and Coolangatta. We spent days away from the beach preparing the venues for each night. Dance music blasted at paint-peeling volumes, alternating with live folk music and bands. Various experts convened discussions on topics useful to teens, some of which included Christian messages of varying subtlety.

In 1966, we called this "Cabaret". Later we renamed it "The Village".

A few years earlier, two friends and I had formed a Kingston-Trio-flavoured folk group: the New Road Trio. Paul Mills played banjo,

Ron Goward played 6-string guitar, and I had a 12-string Maton (just like the Seekers). In the Sixties there were lots of late Sunday night folk venues serving up gospel music of varying competence, execrable coffee and evangelism-lite. The New Road Trio managed to play at one or two every weekend.

We offered our services for part of the Village folk program. "You need a girl," Doc Born suggested.

Judy Beeston sang with her brothers, Graham, older, and Jimmy, younger. Graham, Judy and Jimmy (eponymously known) sang gentle, sweet two-part harmonies. The Swedish folk duo, Nina and Frederick, contributed a substantial part of *GJ&J*'s repertoire. I admired their sound. It had a smoothness that contrasted with our trio's ruggedness. I thought her voice would give us a distinct sound.

Judy turned out to be willing if undemonstrative about the invitation. We rehearsed, joked and smoothed out our fresh sound. I liked it. She made a difference, but primarily to me.

I had girlfriends before Judy, but she was different. What grew out of the relationship between Judy and me was new. Until that time at the Village, I had flirted with girls I thought would make me look good. Self-serving, self-promoting relationships. Not that I had the insight to characterise my behaviour in that way.

But with Judy, novel factors were in play.

First, we started out as mates. A common task drew us together. The three-man one-woman version of the New Road Trio. We were co-workers in a musical enterprise.

Second, we talked. Five decades on, I cannot recall a single deep and meaningful conversation with any girlfriend before Judy. This, despite one of my relationships enduring over two years. I remember her name. I can picture where she lived. I know what she looked like (but then I have photos). What else? Not much. Maybe not even *anything*.

Judy and I had paddocks of common ground. Similar families. Music. Growing up in church youth life. And while she was Presbyterian and I Methodist, the two denominations were already talking up uniting. We achieved it before they did. And more successfully perhaps.

Complementing this common ground were all the ways we were, and are, different. Distinct personality types that balance my weaknesses with her strengths. And the other way, too. I sensed in her a vulnerability, an anxiety that I could balance with my unreasonable confidence. And also, a steady cautiousness that could balance my impetuosity.

This was love of an unfamiliar kind and I only understood it slowly, as it revealed itself in a relationship in which we were each wanting the best for the other. After over five decades together, we agree, we complete each other.

Perhaps this is everyone's experience. If so, it's no less remarkable for being common. In the full flush of early adult love, something began to change in me. Maybe this is part of maturing from teenager to adult. We realise we're not the centre of the world. That, despite the insistence of modern advertising, it's not all about me. That there might be fulfilment in trying to walk in other's shoes. That there might be satisfaction in the success of others.

It would take time for this new awareness to shape my behaviour outside of the narrow confines of Judy and me, but I had plenty of time. For a start, I had finally graduated Year 12. On my second try.

Now, I needed a job.

* * *

6

Honor The System And It Will Work For You

One week into my first paid employment, at nineteen, with a scintilla of previous work experience, I joined the bottom rung of the corporate ladder with the National Bank of Australasia (now better known as NAB). I was about to learn to be the tiniest ant in the banking nest.

I began work in PR. In an open office on the floor above the glory of the 19th century banking chamber, I sat with each day's newspapers delivered to my desk. *The Courier-Mail. The Telegraph.* My job was reading the papers. If I came across any item "which would interest the bank", I would cut it out and paste it on a foolscap sheet. That was the entire job. I suppose someone collected these sheets. I don't recall. I remember the work as mind-numbing. But soon the Bank sent me off for basic training.

For three days I found myself back in a classroom and enjoying myself again. The bank's processes were a labyrinth to learn, solve and negotiate. I loved it. I've never forgotten the Slip G. A green form with multiple uses. Filling out its details correctly became a matter of personal pride. If I honoured the system, it would cooperate with me. If I marked any part of it wrongly, the system would object.

Some years later at World Vision, I recalled this training. I had accepted a position as Executive Team Leader, reporting to the CEO, Harold Henderson. It was an odd position of powerlessness, but more of that later.

For four years prior, I had been setting up a new World Vision office in Hong Kong. One part of my work had been writing a database program on our first IBM PC. It had worked, after a fair bit of debugging, and I thought I understood this emerging world of computing. What I didn't understand was how different a small office with a few personal computers might be from a larger deployment.

When I arrived in my new role in Melbourne, the IT Manager gave me a password to the computer system. With no training. I booted up my terminal (never had one of those before). I saw a menu. One of the menu options read "Run Reports". I selected it. I expected to see a report appear on the screen. Nothing happened.

Next morning, the very outraged IT Manager came into my open plan office demanding to know "Which idiot ordered these reports?" She carried a pile of Z-fold printouts about the size of a suitcase. I apologised for my naivete.

At the NAB, I learned that respect for the system produces right results. Even doing things right-first-time proved satisfying.

A month later a transfer came to Geebung, close to home. It was a minor branch, one of a soon-to-die breed, with three staff—manager, teller and clerk (me). My job was to learn and use the Burroughs machine that put the day's transactions into people's accounts, recording entries onto their statements, and into the bank's records. For one hour of the day, I got promoted to Teller while he had lunch.

Later I wound up in the reverential air of the main banking chamber in Queen Street where I alternated teller duties with carrying packages of cheques up and down Brisbane's main street to the central banking swap house. This also had the advantage of being able to eat lunch on the lawn of Anzac Square with Judy who worked in a nearby solicitors' office.

The bank helped me to learn about organisational life in a proper business, but it taught me little about management or leadership. Most of the people I worked with were grunts just like me, or low-level supervisors. Their only interest was in serving the system. Getting it done.

On 22nd April 1968, I embarked on my second career. My job title was *Fast Phil, the Farmers' Friend*.

* * *

7
Systems Work, If You've Made The Right Assumptions

Queensland's Sunshine Coast in the Sixties was in transition. Sugar was still its major industry, but tourism was edging out the cane fields. The major town was not Maroochydore or Caloundra, but the town with the sugar mill, Nambour. The cane trains owned main street during crushing season, when the cloying scent of molasses dominated for months.

"How do you put up with that smell?" I asked after my first week at Radio 4NA Nambour.

"What smell?" replied Pat Maher, my Manager. "I smell nothing."

And he was right. After two weeks, the scent of molasses evaporated. Or, I suppose, my nose had become accustomed to it. I was becoming a native. There was a lot more to learn.

First, I had to survive initiation. I arrived on a Tuesday and learned how to use the equipment. I practised for most of Wednesday in Studio 2 with an audience of one: me.

At 6pm I entered Studio 1 for my first shift. John McCormack, the Assistant Manager, hovered. For 45 minutes John observed me introducing records, telling the time, pressing buttons on the cassette machines to play commercials and jingles. I was nervous as I had ever been, but after half an hour John seemed to think I was OK to fly solo.

"OK, you're doing fine," he encouraged. "Just remember, start the radio serial on the dot of 6:45 and then it will finish in time for the seven o'clock news."

The radio serial was, even then, ancient. *Dad and Dave* came from the radio era of my parents. It came on a sixteen-inch disc, larger even than today's vinyl LPs. I was about to discover something else strange about it.

After I set the last music in motion, it was *Dad and Dave*'s turn.

I placed the *Dad and Dave* disc on the turntable, lowered the needle into the outermost groove and, now feeling very professional, spun the disc by hand and waited to hear a sound indicating the start.

The needle slid sideways off the disk and bounced once, potentially expensively, on the desk. Thinking I was doing it wrong, I tried again. Same result. As soon as I turned the disc, the needle slid right off.

Stupidity is repeating the same action and expecting a different result. I tried a third time. Bounce.

I looked at the clock. One minute to go and *Dad and Dave* must start. I looked towards the control room. John was standing on one side looking at some gauges. He looked my way as I yelled his name. Radio studios are well sound-proofed. John appeared to lipread.

He came through the double doors.

"Dad and... Needle... bounce," I spluttered.

He walked around behind me. "Oh yeah," he said. He took the needle and placed it in the *middle* of the disc. Found the start, and at the perfect moment, set it in motion. As the opening music of the radio serial played to our listeners, I watched in amazement for the next fifteen minutes as the tone arm tracked slowly *backwards*—from the centre of the disc to conclude at its outer edge. Just in time for the seven o'clock news.

Here was a true antique. A record produced before the outside-in recording method became standard.

"Sorry about that," John said. His sorrow was undermined by the silent applause of my fellow announcers now appearing through the control room glass. Initiation done.

But there is a lesson here. I had been learning a system designed for 78s, 45s and LPs, the three classes of records I knew from childhood. But the system would not work for these ancient 16-inch backward-trackers. The system's failure was useful for giving the new boy a fright, but it also showed that systems don't last. Because it works today is no guarantee it will work tomorrow.

The job of a radio announcer had been my dream since childhood. I would commandeer Dad's AWA Magictape Tape Recorder and play DJ. I loved technology. Still do. But there was something more about radio that appealed. The *proscenium effect.*

The proscenium is that archway that divides a theatre stage from the audience. The curtain usually descends just behind. It divides the theatre physically, but also in other ways. On one side, we have the audience; on the other, the actors. When the actor walks on stage, the audience understands they are playing a role. They are acting. The actor does not play themselves. I suggest this is true even when the person is playing themselves. For most of us, if called upon to make a speech, contribute to a panel discussion, or compere a concert, we adopt a persona. It might look like me, but it's a form of me adapted for the audience.

At twenty, I had no knowledge yet of *Jungian* personality types. Extroverts, introverts? Who knew? But I knew that I was much more comfortable on a stage in front of hundreds of people, than trying to make small talk at a party. Behind the proscenium, or any socially constructed equivalent of the proscenium, I felt safe. In control. I could reveal just as much of myself as I wanted. A little like writing a book, I suppose. Outside there, in the real world, there were more dangers.

Radio was perfect for me—a technological proscenium of microphones, radio waves, and wireless sets.

Judy and I married later that first year. As a legal secretary she found work in Nambour. We rented a flat and enjoyed life on the Sunshine Coast with many quick visits back to parents in Brisbane.

When it felt right, I posted an audition tape to 4CA Cairns. They offered me the morning slot. We piled all our worldly possessions into our Datsun 1600 and, with Judy nursing an ottoman on her lap, we drove the 1,579 kilometres from the Sunshine Coast to Cairns.

In Cairns, a piece of fried coral trout cost 20 cents. Red Emperor was 2 cents extra. We rented a flat a short walk from downtown Cairns for $11 a week. Judy again worked as a legal secretary and I enjoyed radio. AWA paid me $42 a week. I added copywriting to my resume, and commentating on the Queen's visit. We bought a caravan, swapped our Datsun for a Valiant, and moved to a park with other itinerant hippies. We bought a black kitten with white socks. We named her *Whitie*.

Radio differed from working in the bank because the boss, and the audience, tested your performance every day. Lacklustre work, careless panel operation, dreaded dead air, all were immediately clear and widely heard, particularly by management. I embraced this exposure without resentment. I could say much about this, but our story has a long way to go.

Let me describe two incidents in performance evaluation that stick in my memory still. They show two distinct ways to handle performance failures. And two different kinds of leadership—one at 4NA Nambour, the other at 4CA Cairns—one much better than the other.

At 4NA Nambour, the announcers selected their own music from the station library. There were guidelines and a rotating format to follow, but within these strictures there was a certain freedom. One day I exercised rather too much freedom.

I am a fan of harmony singing. In the Sixties, the *Beach Boys* were a favourite. One Saturday on the afternoon shift, I discovered a B-side that contained an *a capella* rendition of "The Lord's Prayer". It's a stunningly beautiful thing—*Beach Boys* layered voices folding into a labyrinth of harmonies. I played it.

Weekends in the studio were lonely affairs. No-one was in the office. I had a six-hour shift interrupted only by an occasional need to answer the phone. As the last chord of the *Beach Boys* faded away, Pat Maher, the Station Manager, barged through the studio doors. He looked furious and stood staring at a point on the wall above my head while I quickly segued into the next record.

"Can I have that?" he said in a tight voice, indicating the Beach Boys' disc in my hand.

I handed it over. Pat produced a letter opener and calmly scored the disc surface, rendering it unplayable. He handed it back to me and left.

For a moment, I didn't breathe. I was appalled at this act of musical vandalism. Had my station manager just slashed the Mona Lisa, I could not have been more stunned.

In Pat's opinion, the *Beach Boys* singing "The Lord's Prayer" was not suitable programming for a summer Saturday afternoon. Perhaps he thought the *Beach Boys* singing a famous Christian song sacrilegious. He never explained himself. Pat just allowed his actions to speak, and they were efficacious. No-one played that record again.

Flip forward, a thousand miles North and two years more experience, and my 4CA Cairns Station Manager, Colin Barrett, called me into his office. He wanted to tell me how disappointed he was. He had a list of things he had noticed about me and my performance. He didn't read out his list but spoke about his expectations of me. He appeared to have a high opinion of my ability. He described me as "talented". This is going well, I thought.

Then he asked, "Do you think you are living up to my expectations?"

Colin mentioned one minor disappointment. "You know if Rod did that, I wouldn't be surprised," he said. I agreed silently that Rod, one of our junior announcers, was hopeless.

"But you?" he looked confused. "You're better than that."

Whether or not I was better than Rod, after this I certainly tried to be. That is the power of expectations. Of carrot, not stick.

* * *

8

Radio Daze

After life in the Sunshine, I landed a slot on Brisbane radio.

It's dark at 5am. My little Honda 90 motorcycle, hardly larger than a scooter, took me through the meandering roads of hilly Brisbane each Saturday morning for the Breakfast shift. 4BK lived on the third floor of the old Queensland Newspapers building in Queen Street. Some years later, the Myer Emporium moved from across the road and all that remains today is the building's facade, overlooking excellent coffee and meals in the Queen Street mall.

Saturday early. Three hours of me, music and commercials. A U-shaped desk with three felt-covered turntables, four cartridge machines, a microphone suspended from the ceiling, and a metal panel about the size of a suitcase placed centrally—the control centre of dials, toggle switches and two prominent VU meters. Across the room stood an interview table with two chairs, a ribbon mike and a cough button for muting the mike if you needed to clear your throat. I don't recall anyone ever using it.

There were four studios in the building's rear overlooking Elizabeth Street. Three studios shared a common airlock with windows on every side. The walls were tinged yellow with the nicotine of five decades of smoking DJs. We sat with our backs to the street, and faced into the Control Room where, if we were lucky, a tech was on duty.

On my right, through the glass, was "Studio Two" which was no longer used, except for commercial production. An old *Rönisch* piano sat covered and never used against one wall. I offered to take it off the station's hands for a pittance, painted it shiny white and enjoyed playing it at home for the next ten years. That piano now lives in the World Vision auditorium in Burwood East. Last I saw the instrument, they had restored it to its former walnut glory. It needed tuning.

I'm not sure whose idea it was for me to play "progressive country music" from 1pm to 4pm, Monday to Friday, but folk and modern country were my music *faves*.

Even those of us who lived in 1970s Brisbane described it as "a big country town". People from New South Wales and Victoria commonly referred to Queensland as the "Deep North." The State Premier was a peanut farmer. Progressive Country music was a good fit. And Festival Hall was just down the road.

On the corner of Albert and Charlotte Streets, stood a 4,000-seat auditorium. An apartment block, *Festival Towers*, replaced it in 2003. Through the Festival Hall stage door walked a pedigree of international entertainers. Many dropped in for an on-air chat. Often, I would return the favour by compering their shows. Whether it was Cilla Black or Glen Campbell, *Andrae Crouch & the Disciples* or *Status Quo*, Roger Miller or Cliff Richard, they were all nice. Ordinary folk mostly doing extraordinary things with their talents.

In my mid-teens, Dad had surprised the family by taking us to hear *Peter, Paul and Mary* at Festival Hall. Sitting high on the cheap seats at the side, I may have been able to spot Judy, my future wife, but we were yet to meet. *Peter, Paul and Mary* were folk music gods. Their talents filtered by the lighting, the proscenium effect, and the crisp sound made them larger-than-life.

Meeting *stars* later across a microphone, casually in their understage rooms, or in the wings during the show, introduced them as human, often uncertain about their performances, and usually easy to get on with. Hardly a prima donna among them.

The darkness of Festival Hall is liquid as you stand in the wings in the moment before the spotlight. Walking onto stage is just like being in the radio studio. You can't see the audience. The stage seems a private place. I always liked that. I usually had little to do except invite the audience to welcome the performer. The technique is well-known and easy-to-deliver. Start soft, build up, say the name as a climax. The audience invariably delivers a wave of satisfying, even thrilling, applause. Job done. Enjoy the show. Free seats my reward for kicking off.

There was life outside radio. Judy and I bought our first house in Ferny Hills. I went back to University and completed an Arts degree majoring in Journalism and Language of the Media. The afternoon program rated well enough for management to mostly leave me alone.

By 1976, I had completed an undergraduate degree, and been promoted to the Drivetime shift. Within a few months, I started my *third career*.

* * *

9

Babyhood Changes You For Good

In the meantime, we became parents. Twice. Our route to parenthood was by a road less travelled.

The contraceptive pill had been around for nearly ten years. Its side-effects were not pleasant. Judy-on-the-Pill was a monthly pantomime of evil-sounding vomiting, unpleasant to the ears and no fun for the victim. In the second year of our married life, during an excursion with Judy's parents from Cairns to Cooktown, Judy set a world record of 24 bathroom visits. Over breakfast the next morning, Judy's mum announced, "You're going off that Pill!" and a grey-faced Judy complied.

The next step was to produce a few perfect children. How many? Judy never considered any limitation. I just never considered the matter. Naively, we thought one just stopped taking the Pill, kept up the sex and instant baby production occurred.

Instead, we were counting days towards optimum fertility. Each failed month grew a weight of anxiety over us. We consulted doctors who proclaimed Judy a fine specimen of baby-making material and ordered sperm counts, the outcome of which was a marginality that did nothing for my confidence. Time passed, and a creeping dark worry became a feature on the edges of our home life.

By the time we rolled our caravan into Brisbane we remained unpregnant. New jobs kept us busy. We sold our caravan but kept the Chrysler Valiant that had faithfully towed it 1,800 kilometres from Cairns. With help from parents and a building society, we bought a house in Ferny Hills and scrounged furniture.

My job in the beginning involved reading news at 9am on our Darling Downs relay, hosting a music program from 9 to 11 and then switching to a talk-back program from the Brisbane station. Various guests rocked up to the neighbouring studio to debate or inform listeners. One day, someone came to talk about adoption.

Adoption. It sounded so easy. Some forms to fill out. Waiting period: 9-10 months. Just like being pregnant. Background information provided. Children matched to parents.

Why not? When my shift was over, I walked down Queen Street to the Adoptions Office and came away with a set of forms.

It was a day of high drama for other reasons. Judy's older brother, Graham, had arrived unexpectedly from Sydney, to announce that his wife had left him. The family had spent the day together at the Beeston home in Moorooka, on the other side of Brisbane. Perhaps to take his mind off harder matters, Graham asked to see our home. They picked me up *en route*.

Later, when we were alone in the house, I showed Judy the adoption forms.

Husband Of The Century! What a contrast from the day's sadness. Suddenly things shifted. Children in the house might be possible. And soon. Judy was over-the-moon.

That night she couldn't sleep. At 2am she slipped from our mattress on the bedroom floor and filled out the forms. The next day I added my signatures and lodged our application for a boy.

Preparations occupied part of our lives for the next few months. There were nappies to buy, bottles, teats, extra towels, baby clothes, a pram. All the usual stuff. Prepared. We thought.

The phone rang. He was here. And waiting. We loved Jamie at sight. He came home. Hungry. A bedlam of boiling followed as we realised everything in the house needed sterilising. Judy's mum arrived. I went meekly to work.

It is a truth universally acknowledged that men aren't ready for fatherhood. I was. *Not ready*, that is. Me-time disappeared and never returned. Even in retirement I'm thinking about the kids. And their kids. Love and marriage had taught me that *couplehood* was a new complex world of decision-making, compromise and negotiation. Fatherhood permutated decisions and options as two became three.

With Judy now a full-time Mum, my role as income-producer was clearer. The responsibility didn't weigh on me. I embraced it with pride, while aware now I had a family dependent on me. I discovered space in my mind and in my heart for all of three—me, Judy and Jamie. Those spaces would never shrink. And we would add more spaces as the family grew.

A few weeks after Jamie arrived, Judy visited the doctor.

"I think I may be pregnant," she informed him.

He grinned. "I would not be surprised."

Nine months later and Melanie arrived. We loved her at first sight too. We were a family of four.

Fortunately, in Judy I had found a life partner who had been in love with babies since she wasn't much older than a baby herself. Judy was a family legend. If there was a baby around, it would be in her arms. Naturally, when we started a family, we did it in a rush. Two babes within ten months. We could see ourselves prefiguring the "Nineteen kids and Counting" family within a couple of decades. That dream (or nightmare) didn't happen. After the initial burst of fecundity, we had a long wait for our third child, Richard.

Much to my genuine surprise, and absolute delight, I loved being a father. A deep paternal love existed unrecognised in my heart. I loved that Jamie became my breakfast buddy, chewing the corners of my vegemite toast while we listened to Malcolm T. Elliott on 4BK. I loved cradling Melanie while she turned out her lights into slumber. It was good to be Dad.

By the time Jamie and Melanie were ready for kindergarten, I was casually looking for fresh career opportunities.

* * *

Book 2
Just Managing

10

Your Work Is A Serious Business

Communications Person. That was the headline on the Positions Vacant page. A description followed with the experience their favoured communications person would have. The career trajectory looked familiar. Media. Writing. Photography. Production. Were they looking for me?

World Vision Australia was looking for a Communications Person. But who, or what, was *World Vision*? A tagline told me "World Vision Australia is a Christian humanitarian organisation." Only a few weeks before I had heard my own voice speaking about World Vision. The *40 Hour Famine*. First time in Queensland. I had read their community service announcements on the radio. Apart from that, I knew nothing about them. In 1976, World Vision was not yet a household name.

Judy and I discussed the job. My resume was soon on its way to Melbourne. Did someone interview me on the phone? I can't remember.

Surely the invitation to fly to Melbourne ("We'll pay your fare") didn't just come in the mail.

What did I expect? A *Christian* organisation? A few volunteers. Old typewriters. Shabby offices in some run-down church hall in the outer suburbs?

Wrong. On the 11th and 12th floors at the corner of Elizabeth and Little Collins Street in the Melbourne CBD, about fifty staff were hard at work. With IBM Selectric typewriters, an up-to-date donor management system (paper-based, but this was 1976), and people with specialised backgrounds. Like me.

I found a professional organisation that was also Christian. It was the nearest thing I could imagine to the experiences with Village discos, MYF and Secondary School Camps. These people were doing it full-time. And being paid for the pleasure. Pinch. Real.

The interview must have gone well. A few months later, the four of us loaded the roof rack on our tiny Honda Civic for the trek to Melbourne—the home of Australian television. We saw the streets of Collingwood and Fitzroy on our TVs every night. It felt like moving to Hollywood. When eventually I visited Hollywood, the myths had been punctured by discovering that Collingwood was just like Parramatta or Fortitude Valley.

The amazing thing about World Vision was this combination of Christianity and professionalism. They took their business seriously. The way they knew the right place to advertise. The way the office was in central Melbourne. They were a business, needing to be near the services that business needed.

Surrounding me in my new location were people who had come into World Vision from business backgrounds. Harold Henderson, the CEO, had been the general manager of Wesley Central Mission in Sydney, an organisation with a multi-million-dollar budget in the welfare sector. I reported to David Longe, the Communications Director. He had come from the Anglican Information Office in Sydney.

My colleagues in the Communications Department included a Graphic Designer and a Radio Journalist carrying an AJA union card. I flashed him my Actors Equity affiliation.

Yet, at the foundations was a Christian vision of the world. World

Vision wasn't a church: it was an aid agency. It supported projects of human development and relief because it believed God wanted to show his concern for the world and its people. One may debate how reasonable this is, but the people in this organisation were entirely reasonable about it. People talked about the work, and about the reasons for the work. They encouraged a freedom. Faith was debated. Rarely with heat.

I didn't get a raise in salary to join World Vision. I got a door to a career path, even though it was hard to see on Day One.

* * *

II

Begin With A Vision

My boss, David Longe, was in turns inspiring and frustrating.

Legends continue about his ability to have "great ideas" while having his morning shower. The legends were true. David would often call me into his office soon after the day started.

"I had this brilliant idea in the shower this morning. Why don't we…"

Some of these ideas were brilliant. *All* of his ideas were to be explored. My natural tendency to want to see how the processes and systems might work was a natural foil for his wilder imaginations. Not that he ever seemed constrained.

The organisation had just completed the pilot of the first *40 Hour Famine*. World Vision tested the Eastern States in turn. The result, in fundraising terms, had been disappointing. The mood from the accounting staff was bleak. It tempts one to say, "As usual." From an accounting point of view, they were right. The three pilots had cost as much to run as they raised in donations. Yes, folks. 100% administration overheads. A fundraising disaster.

David and I had long talks together. He talked long. He was convinced the *40 Hour Famine* could work. There was an economy of scale issue. I won't take the credit, although it sounds like something I might have suggested. Soon, David and I were in a senior staff meeting.

"We've decided," David didn't ask for permission unless pressed, "that the problem is lack of vision. We will take the *40 Hour Famine* national."

This was folly, according to those who had the numbers. But we had come armed with our own numbers that showed that, had we run the Victorian pilot as a single event across the whole country, it would have worked. Economy of Scale. Maybe.

We took it national. David said, "Let's get the Prime Minister to endorse it." Even I thought that would be a stretch, but Malcolm Fraser was happy to oblige. Perhaps he saw the benefit in image terms, the Dismissal still a raw nerve in the electorate. All the television stations of the nation broadcast his endorsement. I learned later, of course, that Malcolm Fraser was passionately concerned about world need. A decade on and he was chair of CARE Australia, an explicit statement.

David noticed that January was a slow time for advertising, but television stations still had to fill up those advertising holes with something. Endless promos weren't enough. So, we launched a special campaign in January, fronted by Senator Neville Bonner. Not a few people told us it wouldn't work. But people apparently watch television, even on holiday.

My job was to translate these greater ideas into action with the collaboration of our small team, and the Sydney-based advertising agency, Pilgrim. It was mind and talent stretching work. I revelled in it.

Another of David's visionary challenges was the one "to make World Vision a household name." Our name recognition was non-existent in 1976. Within a decade, all that changed. By the late 1980s, World Vision was the biggest and best known of all the aid agencies. Our use of television was a key piece of the strategy. TV and radio were mandated to provide free "community service announcements". We produced professional spots for them to use. Most did.

David left Australia in 1980 to a job with World Vision in Britain. He died young and never lived to see World Vision as a household name. During the 1980s under the leadership of another David, Dave Toycen, the organisation made enormous inroads using television specials, and significantly, writing the *40 Hour Famine* into the scripts of *Neighbours* and *Home and Away*.

I remember when I knew we had succeeded. There was a brilliant late-night comedy/cabaret show on ABC-TV in 1989. *The Big Gig*. Hosted by Wendy Harmer, the program featured skits, music and some weird stuff. A personal favourite was Jean Kittson's character *Candida*. One night, Candida spoke of her "World Vision-sponsored child". She knew that everyone in the audience knew what she meant. World Vision Sponsorship had become a brand. A household name. Thanks for the vision, David Longe.

My focus during this time was purely on marketing. Our criterion was return on investment. Dollars raised for dollars spent. If it worked, we liked it. Other voices, more outside than inside World Vision in those days, sometimes questioned our techniques. Following an American model of fundraising allowed some critics to brand us as "too American". Others, more thoughtful perhaps, worried about the way we were portraying Third World poverty. Within our department, we were smugly dismissive.

"You should look at this," David said, presenting me with a hardback book of winning graphic designs in advertising.

I looked. There was a fundraising ad that had a tagline "A Dog In America Eats Better". Brilliant, I thought. It accurately summarised the rich/poor divide. Americans, and Australians, spent more on pets than providing aid and help to the world's poor. In the late 1970s, the ratio was about two to one. Foreign aid somewhere about half what we spent on our pets.

Armed with this statistic, and unencumbered by too much moral or ethical doubt, I turned the tagline into a headline. Placed over a stark black-and-white image of an emaciated child, the advertisement appeared in newspapers and magazines all over Australia. "A Dog in Australia Eats Better."

It made quite a splash.

Offended pet owners bombarded World Vision with venomous letters, phone calls and cans of dog food—a response I thought showed creativity. The offence operated on many levels. Some pet owners didn't appreciate the guilt of their own privileged place in the world being exposed, not to mention that of their pets. Others were offended by linking a child with a dog.

Others liked our bravery. Sometimes hinting at a certain foolhardiness, they commended us for exposing the offensiveness of the gap between the riches of Australia and the poverty of the Third World.

Within the Communications Department, we counted the costs. Then we counted the income. Whatever it takes, was my credo.

I still had some things to learn, and Harold and David were not slow in giving me opportunities. UNESCO proclaimed 1979 as the International Year of the Child. David Longe hitched World Vision's wagon to the UN's train with a proposed tour of the Korean Children's Choir. After a first visit to the World Vision Music Institute in Seoul, Korea, David handed me the production reins. I put to work everything I had learnt at Methodist camps and youth events. Wisely, my first task was to hire well.

David Longe, who revelled in expressing his showman's sensibility, looked after the show content. A friendly morning chat in Geoff Hales' Dandenong Ranges eyrie, engaged him for the music arrangements. EMI agreed to release an LP of the program content. Jillian Fitzgerald, well-known in television for her choreography, agreed to work with us and to spend a fortnight with the choir in Seoul rehearsals.

I went looking at the logistics. We wanted concerts in Perth, Adelaide, Melbourne, Brisbane and at the Sydney Opera House. We had to transport, house, feed and keep contented, twenty-five choristers aged 9 to 16, a half dozen carers, and a similar number of musos. Venue contracts required negotiation. Unions wanted satisfaction.

Moving in and out of my periphery since Brisbane Coffee Shop days was David Smallbone. Originally the bass player for another folk group, David had helped shaped the career of gospel group *Family*. Later he had worked with M7 Records and, just before I left Brisbane radio, David turned up at 4BK to work on promotions. Now he agreed to manage the tour. What a godsend!

I could write another book about that one tour. Cross-cultural complications exacerbated musical differences, logistical failures and personality clashes. Yet, when the curtain rose, all was bliss. The audiences were warmly enthusiastic. The choristers professional beyond their years. The music divine. Thanks to David Smallbone's connections, the publicity train worked. The choir appeared on television and in the papers everywhere. World Vision had a place in the Year of the Child, and the number of people who called themselves *Child Sponsors* swelled.

A year later, I coproduced a packaged telethon. Intended for rural television, which, in those days of freedom, broadcast the occasional program that did not originate from Sydney or Melbourne. The telethon was a three-hour pre-packaged program of entertainment and documentary. Famous folk of the time appeared and endorsed the product: World Vision's work. Live crosses to a phone room in the local TV studio provided local content.

The end product was pleasing, but it never took wing. Broadcast only once, despite my strenuous in-person salesmanship across a few thousand kilometres of travel from Port Pirie to Mackay. There was interest. A few close agreements. But only one taker. The TV station in Renmark ran it with success, but without further exposures the program soon ran past its use-by date.

All, however, was not lost. Every failure is a learning experience and within a few years, World Vision, under the leadership of a new Communications Director (Dave Toycen), Producer (Warwick Olson), and Advisor (Bruce Gyngell), World Vision experienced phenomenal success with the format.

* * *

12

Work With Experts–
Listen And Learn

African night, 1979. The Mercedes-Benz taxi was years older than its driver; his cabin perfumed with diesel from a senescent motor, refusing to die. I had been hours in planes. Melbourne. Overnight in Singapore. A little shopping for bargains. Bombay. Now Kenya. We rattled and bumped from Nairobi airport, through blind streets. Nairobi looked like a country town. We passed a few cityblocks of taller buildings and were in jungle again. Not bush. Jungle. Africa.

Through an impressive gate. Lights ahead illuminated a substantial building, the Serena Hotel. Ossie Emery, my travelling companion, announced: "Welcome to the Serena. Five African Stars accommodation."

"African stars? What's the exchange rate?"

"Oh, about three Aussie stars. Maybe three-and-a-half." He was grinning. Ossie often grinned. Full of good humour. An old hand at navigating foreign places. My first visit to Africa. Ossie had lost count of his. In time, I would too.

At the back of the taxi, I reached for my suitcase and Ossie put a gentle hand on my arm.

"Don't take this man's job away from *him*." He nodded towards the liveried porter.

"What?"

"Don't take this man's job away from him."

Later, across breakfast, Ossie explained.

"We're Australians. We're used to carrying our own bags, but here, this is his job. Not many people here have jobs. We should let him do his job and thank him for it."

I learned a lot because my boss, David Longe, suggested Ossie and I travel to Kenya.

"We need pictures and stories," David summarised.

A simple job description. Ossie for pictures. Me for words. I was yet to discover that Ossie was an exceptional photographer. More than that, he was a first-rate cinemaphotographer, one of the first recognised by the Australian Cinemaphotographers' Society. Entitled to add A.C.S. to his name on film credits.

But more than that, Ossie was a gentle, thoughtful and fun guy. I was blessed to have such a travelling companion. He was an inveterate storyteller. Some of his stories were chapters long and a single journey, or a single meal, might finish before the climax. An hour, or sometimes a day later, Ossie would drop into the conversation a sentence like this: "So I said to the guy with the flamingo under his arm…" and my job was to link this back to the flamingo story from two hours ago. Or maybe last night.

Ossie also liked to wonder. The Rift Valley in Kenya is a vast scar. Aptly named, it is the result of continental drift. People live there, of course. Many of the Maasai variety. Not many houses. Except there was one house in the distance with an orange roof. Ossie gazed through the shimmering heat and wondered.

"I wonder why that guy painted his roof orange?"

But wondering wasn't enough. Ossie reckoned it was an "Aussie thing" to ask such questions. It certainly was an *Ossie* thing.

"Maybe he got a discount on a job lot of paint," he suggested and looked at me. My job was to evaluate the odds of him being right, and suggest an alternative.

"Maybe he just likes orange?"

"You think? Hmm."

"OK. Maybe Civil Aviation asked for his house to be a navigation point."

"Oh. (pondering) Better."

This could go on for a while until Ossie remembered a story.

Despite having a degree in journalism, I didn't think of myself as much of a writer. My craft to date had been predominantly copywriting. Complete stories were a step up.

I had a notepad, and I used it. Questions and answers. Often a question or two from Ossie who, unlike me, had been around the block a few times. Getting the quotes. Checking the spelling. "How do you spell Maasai?" No-one could agree then. Or now. I wrote fourteen stories which worked out to about one a day.

At the end of the first day, I asked Ossie to read my story. "Very good," he said, handing me back the pages.

"Really? I can never tell if my writing is any good."

The puzzled look on Ossie's face was the greatest gift to an uncertain writer.

"Well, that's a surprise, but I don't think you need to worry," he said. "Until you see the pictures, anyway."

The pictures, in beautiful black and white, were all superb.

The African regional office organised our itinerary to World Vision projects. We visited two amazing Kenyan women, of the English settler variety, who had spent a decade or more driving a VW Kombi around distant villages to tell them about Jesus. The experience had taught them an important lesson in development. *Give me a fish, I eat today. Teach me to fish, I eat every day.* Now they had built a training centre for indigenous evangelists.

We spent another day in the Mathare Valley. Sounded romantic. It wasn't. A slum with all the appeal of a garbage dump, yet home to thousands of desperate souls.

The beginnings of small enterprise loans schemes. In Bahati, a man who World Vision assisted to market his "better broom". Using coconut fibres, wood and wire, he made a broom that would last twenty times longer. With eight children and a wife to feed, he was selling them for two Kenyan shillings and making 25% profit on each.

Water would soon come to Kima, a village in need of a dam.

Parents in Ngelani were trained to administer a vocational training centre. An agricultural project at Homa Bay was adding variety and certainty to crops.

White folk ran nearly all these projects. Many of them foreigners. Still naïve in the world of development aid and the history of colonisation, I found this natural and unremarkable. None of my stories noted it. The Kenyan Kombi women, however, were signalling a different future in which the empowerment of local people might become intentional. Even a decade later I hadn't quite tapped into how the locals really felt about us.

I confronted the issue on my second visit to Mogadishu, Somalia. Ten years on, and I had a *60 Minutes* crew for company. Their reporter was Prime Minister, Bob Hawke, recently retired from politics by Paul Keating's machinations, and not well pleased about it.

A decade earlier, Mogadishu had been an attractive coastal city with rooftop restaurants bordered with spectacular bougainvillea and cool, shaded courtyards to rest in during the waning evening heat. Now the city was at war with itself. Young men with weapons decorated the trays of trucks. These mobile squads were called "technicals". Moving around town required a careful choice of *technical* friends. One did not want to arrive at a war zone with the wrong gunmen on your truck.

Amid the mayhem, World Vision was providing healthcare and shelter to displaced families. A food store became the scene for a confusing rant from a tall, angry man. The television crew had inevitably attracted a crowd. Most were merely spectating, but as I walked out of camera shot, this man was suddenly in my face. Yelling. He towered over my 1.8 metres and showered me with words I did not understand, but a meaning that was as clear as the African sunshine.

He was not happy with me. He was not happy with the film crew. His finger waved and then pointed at the bridge of my nose. I'm sure I went cross-eyed for a moment. I took a step backwards.

Within seconds, someone else in the crowd jostled him away.

"What was that all about?" I stuttered to our Somali interpreter.

"He doesn't want you here. This is Somalia. These problems are Somalian problems. He thinks you should go away and let us sort out our problems ourselves."

I wanted to apologise to the man, to explain that I agreed with

Work With Experts—Listen And Learn

him, that we only wanted to help relieve some suffering, that he misunderstood us and our motives.

But our motives were not always quite this pure. There always was, and perhaps always will be, a sense of a perfect right to help. Manifest destiny. We have the money, the means and we care. Let's help. Sometimes we asked some local authority if that was OK with them. Sometimes they might say yes, only because it improved their hold on power.

This has changed in my lifetime. The language of aid has become enhanced with ideas of development, recovery, empowerment. And, these days, these words are more in evidence. The visual evidence? Fewer white faces.

But, back in the 70s, our leadership in Africa was mostly white and mostly foreign. We met Dr Ken Tracey, World Vision's boss in Africa. Ken used to be a missionary dentist. He had left New Zealand long before and now had his hands full developing our work in the vastness of Africa. Ken, Ossie and I hit it off immediately and became lifelong friends. Ken was soon to take up a role at the international office and a decade later he would be part of my Australian team. When Ken left Africa, his replacement came from the African continent. More locals followed around the world.

Ossie and I got our story and pictures. An ample supply of words and images for a few more months of feedback to supporters. Only one thing remained. We had to get home. I discovered that I needed a yellow fever vaccination. Really, a typically naïve traveller's oversight. I pled guilty and got the shot in Nairobi.

It took me two weeks to get home. The man at Bombay immigration didn't like my African stamp for Yellow Fever vaccine. I spent a week editing my stories in the Bombay Quarantine Centre (read *jail*) until they were certain I was not an infectious danger to the Indian people.

Still learning.

* * *

13

Manage People– Avoid Power

When David Longe left for Carnaby Street to work for World Vision Europe, I was offered his chair. I now reported as Communications Director to Harold Henderson, the CEO. David's chair came with a new title—a desk, too.

Now I had a team to manage, and not much training in how. Warwick Olson, our partner at Pilgrim Advertising, gifted me with two international immersions. Warwick had previously worked in Switzerland on the Lausanne Congress on World Evangelisation and had a raft of European contacts. He took me to meet them all. A year later he did the same for me in America.

When I asked him why Pilgrim wanted to be so wonderfully generous, he was dismissive. "We're making a lot of money from placing your advertising," he said, "we thought we should give some of it back." That was true, but still generous.

We didn't really have a planned marketing program. We produced a regular magazine for supporters. It produced donations almost without asking. Once or twice a year, when there was media publicity, we would mount an appeal. It seemed rather ad hoc. Warwick's invitation gave me the chance to see how others were doing it.

One huge Christian charity in Britain had just completed a nationwide campaign in churches. They received donations from a million donors. *One million donors!* I thought. *That's a mailing list of one million names!*

Warwick raised an eyebrow, then asked the manager, "What did you do with the names?"

"The names?"

"Yes. Did you follow up with anything?"

"No. Why would we do that?"

I wanted to ask him to give the names to me. I would send thank-you letters to them all—plus a gentle invitation to send a second donation. Someone who has given once is likely to do so again. Especially if thanked.

Also, we met people who were ahead of us. The American Bible Society had a sophisticated communications strategy that included magazines, letters, and appeals. I copied.

While this helped me to develop strategies, implementation required a team. How do you manage a team? I had some fine examples. Not the least my boss, Harold Henderson. He managed me in a way that I felt valued and believed in. There was something of 4CA Cairns' Colin Barrett in his style.

A glance at my diaries for these years shows I was busy. Almost everything I did taught me something. My contact list exploded with media names, marketers, entertainers, politicians, commentators. There were lunches and dinners, many gratis. I joined everything for which I could claim a qualification—the Direct Marketing Association, the Public Relations Institute, the Australian Institute of Fundraising, the Australian Institute of Management. I attended a score of training events.

The international network of communications staff flourished. Soon we were gathering for annual conferences. Invariably, overseas. That gave me the chance to attend conferences of Press Associations and Christian Communicators in the USA.

Manage People—Avoid Power

The work continued. It was all new and exciting. Producing documentaries with Anne Deveson for screening on television took us to Uganda, Somalia, and Ethiopia. With an advertising agency in Sydney, I became familiar with Ansett and TAA.

I enrolled in the first intake of the MBA program with Deakin University. Gradually, I learned theory about things I did intuitively, if not always correctly.

Discovering the power of office architecture was a revelation. It had never occurred to me that tables and chairs could have so much meaning. Placing one's desk in the centre of the room tells a story. Pushing your desk against the wall tells a different story. These things communicate.

At first, I placed my desk facing my door. Staff came and stood in front of me. The desk between us. Soon I worked out that this was a barrier. I turned the desk into the wall. Now staff could come and stand beside me to talk. If we needed to sit, I used low seats around a coffee table. Such slight adjustments became tools for collaboration.

Some managers close the doors of their offices. I never did. Perhaps I closed the door if someone with me was crying, or if the news I was about to share might make them cry. Otherwise, open door policy. My attitude was that the person standing at your door is more important than the one on your screen, or your phone. Still is, despite owning an iPhone.

Sometimes one needs space to concentrate. An interruption-free zone. As my work involved more discussions and conversations, finding time to read, think and write, became more difficult. I found solutions other than closing the door. Shifting my working hours by starting later and finishing the day when the building was almost deserted.

Later as CEO, I routinely worked at home one day a week. I was contactable by phone and email, but absence from the office created less intrusion. The timing blended pleasantly with toddler-raising at home, too. I got a lot of reading done with a two-year-old on my lap.

Now on my first management role, I discovered that information was a key to getting things done. I invented reasons to get people talking to one another. Three regular structures emerged from these conversations. A Staff Meeting to deal with everyday issues of administration and issues as they rose which met weekly, a Strategic Management Team met monthly to look down the track at plans, and a think tank with Pilgrim Advertising and invited gurus which met less often.

I enjoyed this first experience of leading a team. It was small (about twenty staff) well-motivated and friendly. There was at least one exception. An applicant who seemed well-suited to an administrative role, arrived carrying a heavy suitcase of mental health issues. I discovered the tougher part of leadership—the soft and subtle work of managing the people themselves.

Relocation became a feature of this period too. The organisation outgrew the rented premises in the Melbourne CBD. The accountants got out their calculators and proclaimed, "Don't rent. BUY!" We bought, just two tram stops down St Kilda Road.

Soon after we moved in, it was already too small. A renovation at the back of the property, over what had been a carpark, doubled accommodation. No sooner had we moved into this annex than our growth filled it. An eight-storey building came on the market nearby and everyone breathed a sigh of relief as we moved into four floors, keeping the rest for tenants.

We reserved the top floor for a Board room, the CEO and other senior staff. Next lower down were the staff responsible for receipting, called "Gift Management", and the Donor Services team. My team occupied the next floor down. Was it a hierarchy? Doubtless some interpreted it that way.

* * *

14

The Best For God's Work–Stay Grounded

*Just because God can use just anything,
doesn't mean we should give him just anything to use.*
—Anonymous (although I recall saying it).

America is the birthplace of World Vision. When I arrived in 1976, the organisation had started an internal revolution. They called it "internationalisation" because what had started as an office in the USA, now had fundraising entities in Canada, Australia, New Zealand and South Africa. It seemed wise that the Americans should yield some control.

The result was a new organisation—World Vision International (WVI). And a name change for the entity in the United States which now became World Vision Inc. The CEO/President of the American organisation, Dr Stan Mooneyham, became the first President of the new International body.

Stan was accustomed to being known as the "President of World Vision." My boss, David Longe, wanted to position World Vision Australia as an Australian organisation, with an Australian chief executive and governing board.

"It doesn't look right," he said, "if we just call Stan, President of World Vision. It will confuse our supporters about who is boss here. It makes it sound like our boss, Harold, has to report to Stan, whereas Harold reports to our own Board."

I wrote a small announcement in the World Vision magazine about Stan's planned visit Down Under. I gave him a title—International President of World Vision. Apparently, Stan felt slightly slighted. I was puzzled. I wondered what kind of President we had.

The answer came at the airport. Dr Mooneyham came off the plane first. He was a tall, good-looking, smartly dressed man of late middle age in a grey suit. Hair neatly cut, blow-waved and rinsed blue.

Our International President was a member of the blue rinse set. It was not a hair colouring one expected to see on a man in the Melbourne of 1976. *Perhaps blue rinse is normal for blokes in California*, I thought, *but not here*. Our world was more cloistered. Television was black and white, yet to show us America's true colours.

I was soon to hear stories about Stan's penchant for living the Presidential life. He stayed, rumours had it, in the best hotels. He travelled First Class. The suit was probably Italian.

World Vision was a serious business. Was I seeing this ethos being taken too far?

Jim Douglas evidently thought so. Jim was assisting Stan in writing one of his books. They found themselves on the same flight. Stan in First Class: Jim in Cattle. After take-off, a flight attendant came to Jim in seat 56K and presented Stan Mooneyham's business card on which was written:

Jim, please join me in First Class. There is a spare seat for you.

Stan

The Best For God's Work—Stay Grounded

Jim returned the card with his answer:

Thank You Stan. I would prefer to have the grievance.

There was much to admire about Stan Mooneyham that made it easy to cope with his affectations. He was an excellent communicator. An excellent writer. He had gravitas that felt Presidential. And I was to discover he had profound emotional depth. A man with a good heart.

I saw these two sides of Stan as I prepared for my next role in World Vision.

"We need to be doing something in Hong Kong," I told my New Zealand friend in the WVI office.

"How do you mean", asked Ken Tracey.

"Have you seen how much money the US office is raising in Hong Kong? These are people who want so badly to support World Vision, they are sponsoring children through the US organisation. Sending bank transfers across the Pacific! World Vision should set up an office. A World Vision Hong Kong."

"Write me a one-page proposal," said Ken, "I'll give it to Stan."

That's how I found myself sent to Hong Kong to set up a new World Vision office, but before that, Stan wanted to chat. I guessed it was a job interview.

Getting an hour with Stan Mooneyham wasn't the easiest logistical exercise when you live on opposite sides of the world, but Ken worked out where our itineraries might coincide.

Amid Stan's permanently peripatetic lifestyle, a three-day window emerged when we could meet. Appropriately it would be in Hong Kong. He was going there for some R&R. I should join him. He would be at the Peninsula Hotel. A room awaited me.

The Peninsula Hotel. I had stayed there once before on Cathay Pacific's ticket. I never thought I would be lucky twice.

Cathay Pacific were major sponsors of the Australian tour by the Korean Children's Choir in 1979. In return for prominently displaying Cathay Pacific everywhere we could, they provided air fares for the choir, and a pre-tour visit to Seoul for me and David Longe. *En route*, Cathay Pacific booked us into the Peninsula Hotel. Expensive doesn't begin to characterise this hotel.

Hong Kong is a crowded, busy, noisy city. Trams rattle down major streets. The sound and stench of diesel taxis assault you. Everything is crowded. Air-conditioner units, washing lines and electric cables cling to the walls of apartment buildings, jostling for space with illegal makeshift verandas, giving buildings ravaged faces. Shops spill out onto footpaths, their interiors crammed. Everything looks like a hoarder's hell. Space is money in Hong Kong. Hotel rooms have European rather than American dimensions.

Overlooking the harbour is the Peninsula Hotel. A Colonial relic, but not dead yet. Suite sized rooms. Generously sized foyers and hallways staffed by simperingly attentive staff. A fleet of Rolls Royces piloted by liveried chauffers transport guests from the airport in silent, leather-lined luxury. A shopping arcade within the hotel contains shops in which air occupies more space than wares. There is an entire shop for Chanel. Another for Louis Vuitton. The restaurants are beyond wonderful. Stan had invited me to stay there. I didn't have to pay the bill.

It's a measure of World Vision hubris at the time that few eyebrows twitched, let alone rose. The plain truth is that these privileges are super-seductive and so over-the-top satisfying that all kinds of rationalisation wash away reason. Stan was working hard. His life was not his own. Every day was wall-to-wall work for the International President. He was welcome to some Rolls Royce fuelled relaxation. Entitled, even. Perhaps.

It affected me too. Even when we later lived in Hong Kong, I would walk through the Peninsula Hotel with more than a tinge of regret that I could only justify the occasional purchase of Chanel deodorant. Once I sat in the foyer with Mike Willesee who was a guest between flights. He paid for morning tea.

This is a hard ethical area to get right. And the gap between "not just anything for God" and "only the best for God" is a grey area bordering a slippery slope. Lots of people appreciate World Vision. They like what we do, and how we do it. They want to help. Affluent families offer support, and not only with money. They offer a piece of their privileges.

When James Strong was CEO of TAA, I watched him transform TAA into Australian Airlines and then merge it with Qantas. I was mightily impressed and invited him to come and have a meal with World Vision senior staff. He graciously obliged arriving, not in a Rolls Royce, but in a Holden. OK, it was an HSV Grange, but still a Holden.

Later I found in my mail an invitation to join a secret society. The Qantas Chairman's Club is an airport lounge for the invited. Many Board chairs, chief executives, and all politicians get invited. Apart from spacious and less crowded lounges at airports all over the world, members were first in line for upgrades. When I flew economy class to Sydney, which I did almost every two weeks, check-in staff would invariably swap my boarding pass for business class. Did I object? I did not. I appreciated the gift, which cost World Vision nothing.

I sometimes asked, "What would Jesus do?" The answer was rarely clear. First, I had no pretensions to be Jesus, merely a poor follower. Second, Jesus' behaviour in relation to kindness offered to him was mixed. Since he was without a place to lay his head, he accepted offers. Even his grave was the gift of a rich man. He wasn't to occupy it for long, of course.

Perhaps my middle-class upbringing would guide me through this labyrinth. Effectiveness trumped abstemiousness. Getting the job done was more important to me than checking that everyone had switched the lights off at night.

As for my interview with Stan, it must have gone OK. We only met once during the three days, for a meal in another hotel on Nathan Road. Yes, it was delightful. There was wine. I had retired my temperance pledge by then. Stan was warm, paternal and generously encouraging. On a later visit together to Beijing, one of his last acts with World Vision, he noticed that the Bible I carried was the less-common version called "The Jerusalem Bible." Less common for Evangelical Protestants anyway. I liked the fact that J.R.R. Tolkien had helped in the translation. I felt I could read his influence in the Psalms.

"Can I borrow your Bible?" he asked. I agreed, thinking he just wanted to compare its translation to more common varieties. Instead, he returned it the next day with the following written on the first page:

"Philip—One outstanding joy for me has been to watch you grow as a person and a Christian. Your gifts are large, your skills are keen, your future, by God's grace, is unlimited. I am pleased to know you, to have you as a brother and a colleague, and to <u>celebrate you!</u>

Affectionately,

Stan Mooneyham
17-2-82

* * *

Book 3
Go East Young Man

15

Go To The People, Live With Them, Learn From Them

Culture Shock is not like a car crash. It creeps up on you. Slowly corrodes your foundations. Eating away at the roots of your reality. You don't get Culture Shock on holidays. You get it when you go live somewhere else for a long time. Late in the first year you will reach the stage where every daily activity or social encounter feels unbearable, where you cross the street to avoid conversations with locals, where life is just so hard, and the people are bad-mannered, impatient and unfriendly, and the local ways of doing things are stupid, ludicrous or insane.

Then something amazing happens. You become a local. You find yourself driving like a local. Your ears hear complete sentences in the local dialect. The people are friendlier, nicer, more patient with you. Doing something like a local brings a frisson of enjoyment.

Our family were about to experience living in another culture. Early in 1982 we became foreigners in a foreign place. World Vision asked me to start a new fundraising office in Hong Kong.

The name *Hong Kong* means *perfumed harbour* in its original Chinese. It's an excellent harbour, narrow and long, protected on the ocean side by a steep island, also named "Hong Kong" and referred to locally as "the island". The landward side rises quickly towards Lion Rock.

"Aim the plane at Lion Rock," said the captain of our Boeing Jumbo to his First Officer at the controls. "When the passengers are certain we will hit the mountain, tip the plane suddenly to the right as far as possible. Keep one eye on the runway as you make the turn, and your other eye on the right wingtip and make sure you don't cut through any lines of laundry on top of the apartments near the airport. When you clear the apartments, straighten her up, cut power and drop onto the tarmac."

Kai Tak airport was one of the few airports where a successful landing invariably evoked applause. Before they built the new airport off the back of distant Lantau Island, this was usually your welcome to Hong Kong. If the weather gods were kind, the pilot might come in from the other direction over the harbour, but mostly you got this sudden lurch away from Lion Rock. Whether because of weather, or just because it was more fun for the pilots, I never found out. My family's four-year Oriental sojourn began with this minor culture shock, so different from landing at Tullamarine.

This was a first for Judy, Jamie and Melanie. I was already an international traveller, including visits to Hong Kong. I'd warned the family about the plane's lurch to the right and encouraged the children to watch the wing tip as we landed.

I was aware that first impressions of Hong Kong would be discomforting. Even frightening. We could have plunged right into Hong Kong's maelstrom by booking a room at one of the Nathan Road hotels, but I knew the South side of the island to be much quieter, less crowded and leafier. The Hong Kong International School that the kids would attend was there too.

I relaxed, but Judy was much less sanguine. Some years later while speaking to a women's group, she recalled the moment.

"This was my first trip overseas," she said. "And we had two kids, aged nine and eight, depending on us.

Go To The People, Live With Them, Learn From Them

"*What if...*
   the plane crashes;
   we can't find somewhere to live;
   we can't find suitable food;
   we can't find suitable doctors, dentists, hairdressers;
   we can't find somewhere to worship;
   we can't make any new friends;
What if Chinese rebels kidnap the kids and take them off somewhere to become white slaves?"

Inside the terminal, Judy's first impression of Hong Kong was how neat everyone was. Having left behind the large bellied, Newcombe moustached Customs officers in Sydney, the neatness and uniformity of their Chinese counterparts impressed her.

Outside the terminal it was night. A busy and noisy night. Just like every night in Hong Kong, but not like anything Judy had experienced. People were everywhere. On the move. Traffic noises louder than voices. Taxis horning.

"One of the women from the Hong Kong office met us," Judy continued. "She rode in our hotel car for part of the way until we dropped her in the middle of the busy streets somewhere near her home. I was afraid for her as she disappeared into a bustling crowd. Neon signs in English and Chinese characters were everywhere. My myopic brain couldn't take them in.

"Our hotel was on the island of Hong Kong, so we had to travel through a tunnel under the harbour. I noticed damp patches on the walls and wondered if it was leaking!

"As they escorted us to our hotel room, I tried not to give in to my anxieties. I bravely ignored the huge black cockroach lying dead in the corridor. Later, when we were in our flat, he would return many times to haunt me for being ignored.

"During the night I woke to the sound of sirens wailing, intermingled with the whine of the double-decker buses as they turned outside our hotel to make their slow progress back into town. I vowed I was going back to Australia in the morning!"

As I knew, Judy could worry for Australia.

But then came the dawn. The Repulse Bay Hotel was a grand old establishment from the 1920s, in the tradition of British Colonial living. All the rooms were sizeable, with slow fans in high ceilings, full bathrooms and bay windows that commanded a calming view across the beach and the South China Sea. Judy woke and found herself in paradise.

Melanie pushed past her mother for a look at the view. "A boat, Mummy, a boat!" A two-masted old sailing ship was moored off the beach.

"Mummy, there's a castle too!" announced Jamie, craning past his mother. Sure enough, to her right was a castle, or more probably someone's folly. A sandy beach beckoned her feet. Verdant headlands on left and right framed the view. Maybe she could live here after all.

Questions accompanied the job of setting up a new World Vision entity. How did the legal system work? British in style, but different from Australia. What are the taken-for-granted rules for living? You'll only notice them when you break them. Do I need to know the language? Yes, it's the best insight into how people think. Will my Australian English work here? Sometimes. But it will only be a few weeks before a staff member asks, "Mr Hunt, what is a 'chook'?"

My entry to World Vision Australia was on the bottom rung. I was the copywriter. Over six years they had promoted me to the leadership of a department of about twenty souls, many of whom had once been my peers. Coming up through the ranks left me feeling like I was still with the ranks. One of the boys and girls. This may have been an illusion held only by me, but in Hong Kong it was different. For two reasons.

Within Chinese society there remained respect for age and authority. It's a Confucian notion that has served the Chinese for better and for worse. In my case, it prevented any of the staff I hired from calling me by my first name. I was *Mr Hunt* for the next four years.

Second, I was an outsider. A *gwei-lo* in Cantonese (literally *foreign ghost*, but usually delivered without conscious racism). Not just an outsider, but a visitor. We were not emigrating to Hong Kong. I was there on assignment. Set up the office. Give it systems, shape and an operating culture. Find a local person to replace me. I reported to Hal Barber, Executive Vice President back in California at the International Office and he set no timeline for the journey, but a sunset was in everyone's mind.

I inherited two staff from the program office that had recently

Go To The People, Live With Them, Learn From Them 69

closed—Barbara Tse responsible for the finances, and Elizabeth Li, responsible for everything else. They proved good colleagues and Barbara instructed me in the ways-things-are-done-around-here.

Meanwhile, Jamie and Melanie, our kids, enrolled at the Hong Kong International School, ever after referred to as *H-kiss*. It was an American Lutheran school. The kids enjoyed the cosmopolitan student body, and the ability to converse in English with accents appropriate to the school's nationality. Melanie could soon pass for a *Valley girl*. Considering that three decades later she would live in America, this was a useful skill to pick up.

Judy and I were already used to relying on one another, separated in Melbourne from family supports. Hong Kong cast us further adrift as a family of four. Yet, the exploration of all this foreignness became our fresh adventure.

I launched into Cantonese lessons. But French and German at high school is no preparation for this—the journey from Europe to Asia. I had NO idea. And forget about learning to *read* Chinese. In four years, I mastered the numbers, the characters for the name of World Vision Hong Kong, and the character for Centre because it appeared on the names of buildings. And it is the first character in the word *China*—the Middle Kingdom between Heaven and the rest of us foreign devils.

European languages, I realised, all borrow from one another. And English is the worst offender. But with Chinese I was suddenly unmoored. Tenses? Forget it. Odd sounds added to verbs might give you the idea that an action has been completed, but it didn't seem the same as good old *past tense*. And inflections to indicate meaning? No way. Cantonese has six tones to change the meaning of words. Yes, how you say something changes its meaning. This could have startling outcomes.

The Baptist College class for Cantonese Language met twice weekly for a 90-minute lesson. We occupied a somewhat shabby room in Argyle Street in Kowloon City. I learned early to say "*Ah-gai-lo-gai*" with the right tones. A dozen blow-ins from the foreign missionary world gathered with evident dread for the opening short devotions. Each of us strained to extract meaning from the passing torrent of Cantonese. At least *A-men* sounds much the same in most languages.

Then there would be some teaching with chanted replies, and the occasional individual singled out for special help. I found that music ability helped. We learned to count to ten. "*Yat-yih-saam-sei*" equalled one through four. But while one and four are sung with a flat level tone, two is pitched lower, and three starts high and drops down.

To my right, one older classmate had difficulty with three.

"Miss Pierce, Miss Pierce," interrupted the teacher, "can you try it alone for a moment."

"*Saam*," Miss Pierce replied hitting the high note and staying right on it.

"*Saam*," said the teacher, the word dropped about a 5th in musical terms.

"*Saam*," replied Miss Pierce. Hopeless.

"Stand up on the chair, please," asked the teacher.

"Pardon?"

"I want you to try something. Please stand on the chair."

Miss Pierce, reluctant to perform this undignified request, nevertheless hitched up her skirt and complied.

"Now, try to say *saam* as you step down off the chair."

Miss Pierce looked at the floor, opened her mouth, said "*Saam*" and stepped off the chair in one action. She hit the falling tone. There was applause and laughter—including from a grateful Miss Pierce.

Learning an Asian language revealed something ingrained. I believed that people who didn't speak English well were stupid—or children. I didn't believe this in my head, but it was part of my subconscious—one of the deep-seated prejudices within the Australian born. And not only Australians.

Trying to speak and function in Cantonese cured me of this prejudice. I discovered that, regardless that I had ideas, plans, and sophisticated understandings about human behaviour, it was very difficult for me to communicate anything beyond giving directions to taxi drivers and having a vague sense of overheard Chinese conversations.

At a Rotary dinner I found myself the only non Chinese at the table. They were talking to me as if I were a child. It was a very important lesson for me about the way I relate to people for whom English is not the mother tongue. I realise that anyone who can speak a second language with any kind of fluency is, by no means, stupid.

Learning a non-European language also opened my mind to the way culture is encoded in language. Grammar is based on taken-for-granted assumptions about how things work. For reasons that others can explain better than I, English verbs have tenses that locate an action in time. Present tense, past, future, present continuous, past continuous. These seemed absent in Cantonese. Instead, there were sounds (suffixes if you like) that you added to verbs to show, not time so much, as if you had completed an action. This implied the past tense but wasn't quite the same.

Because Cantonese is a tonal language, inflection hardly exists. An English speaker can say "Really" with different inflections to communicate sorrow, incredulity, surprise, disgust, questioning and more. Again, Cantonese has a bunch of useful sounds you could add to indicate you were asking a question or some other emotion.

There are no words for "Yes" or "No". Instead, one should repeat the verb positively or negatively (rather like the way French speakers use "*ne...pas*"). So, the answer to the question "Are you going to Kowloon?" is "going" or "not going". Although, often one hears "*haih*" in answer to a question which is roughly equivalent to saying "is" in English.

Over time, I got the distinct impression that my Chinese friends experienced time and place differently from me.

"When can we meet?" I would ask.

"Next week sometime," the answer might come. I would hear the phrase "*gum-seung-ha*" and roughly translate it as "sometime", or better still, "ish."

I would then negotiate until we got down to "Next Friday at Golden China Restaurant at 3 o'clock". Except that my friend would always qualify the time. "Three o'clock-ish."

I would be happy to look for this friend when he arrived between 2:55 and 3:20. But this would not do for him.

"You know the Golden China Restaurant inside?" he would ask. I agreed that I did.

"There's a booth on the right side as you come in, near a hat stand, and between two mirrors."

"OK"

"I'll meet you there."

When the appointment came, I could never depend on my contacts being on time, but I always knew where to find them.

Many of my classmates at the Baptist College were foreign Christian workers, and the College expressed its Baptist traditions by attempting to teach us to pray in Chinese. From time to time, the teacher would ask us to pray on behalf of the whole class. Aloud. Fortunately, God understands Cantonese even when spoken by a struggling *gwei-lo*. When my turn came, I felt reasonably prepared. Two sentences would be good enough. Followed by the imprecation "in the Name of the Lord Jesus Christ, *A-men*."

There was only one hitch to my performance. The word for *Lord* in Cantonese is *jyŭ*, the accent over the letter u requiring a rising tone. Unfortunately, when I arrived at "the name of the Lord Jesus" it came out as *jyū*, said with a flat tone, neither rising nor falling.

"Well done, Mr Hunt," the teacher encouraged. "But you may have noticed that Mr Hunt has fallen into a common missionary trap. Did anyone hear it?"

Silence. Then Miss Pierce proved her mettle.

"Did he say, 'Lord Jesus' or 'pig Jesus'?" she offered.

"Yes, I'm afraid he did say 'in the name of the *pig*, Jesus Christ'," confirmed the teacher. "It's a good idea to get that right," he added with a grin.

After three years, I was still not fluent. English speakers suffer a disadvantage. English is spoken just about everywhere, and where it is a second language, people you work with want to use it. For many, ability in English is a ticket to ride.

While there was much Cantonese spoken in our office, especially as the staff grew from three to twenty, no-one ever spoke to me in Cantonese. Partly this was because my replies varied between strange and ridiculous, but mostly because they wanted to hear me speak proper English as part of their personal development. I did not begrudge them the lessons, although I wondered whether my Australian English would be, for them, a career advantage. Most modern English-as-a-second-language speakers prefer a North American lilt.

Little by little we learned the ways. I remembered the word *ethnomethodology* from my one semester of sociology. These are the taken-for-granted rules unique to a local society—the way we do things around here. Hong Kong had many *ethnomethodologies*. As we discovered them, we also discovered the taken-for-granted rules we had brought with us from Australia.

It is in traffic that this first becomes obvious. I had already noted that after colleagues made their first trip to Asia, they would return talking about the traffic.

"The traffic is chaotic."

"They drive like there are no rules."

"Everyone sounds their horn all the time."

"Cows have right-of-way." That one from a first visit to India.

But each place has its own traffic logic, even between cities in Australia. Regardless of the rules, merging is much easier in Melbourne than Sydney. In Australia, we may get annoyed if someone scoots up the emergency lane by a line of stopped cars. Try that in Germany or Switzerland and you will hear German words they didn't teach you in school. You may experience assault.

In Hong Kong, where space is precious, drivers learn to use all of it. When stopped at an intersection, one lane can easily accommodate three or four cars. So why not? People don't queue for buses, but form en masse and then, without difficulty or apparent irritation, filter on board. It just works, and I avoided much wasted anger and anxiety by discovering these ethnomethodologies and abiding by them.

The same was true in the office. I selected our first office in the Peninsula Centre. I recognised the character for *jung* ("centre"). A development was going up in Tsim Sha Tsui East. All brand-new buildings. Rents were reasonable, so I took a two-year lease.

Gradually, I realised the mistake. The Peninsula Centre had an upmarket vibe, more suited to banks and lawyers. It hinted at an American image. The staff felt it was too grand for World Vision Hong Kong. I got the message and when our lease expired, we moved the short distance across Chatham Road into old Kowloon. The office in the oddly named Prat Avenue was no cheaper than the Peninsula Centre, but the address looked a lot better on our letterhead.

By the time we moved to Prat Avenue we had grown to a dozen staff. We expected more growth, so there was plenty of room for all.

"A desk for each person," I suggested. I worried that staff were working two to a desk.

It took two days before the one-person-one-desk rule fell apart.

"Vivien's moved in with Veronica again," I observed to Barbara.

"Yes." Barbara showed no surprise.

"Why?"

"They work better that way." And they did, too. *Like cars at an intersection.*

*   *   *

16

Child Sponsorship Needed Fixing

For $11 a month you can change a child's life.

The best thing about Child Sponsorship was that it worked. World Vision didn't invent child sponsorship. Foster Parents Plan, for instance, was much older. It's a simple idea. Connect a child with a donor. Ask for an agreed monthly pledge. Use that money to clothe, feed, and provide other services to the child. When Bob Pierce, the founder of World Vision, discovered abandoned children in a South Korean orphanage, it worked just fine.

Twenty-five years later, the sponsorship program in World Vision was still working well. But it had its critics.

For starters, most of the children in the program were no longer children sheltered in an orphanage. They were kids living in towns and villages with their families. Looking after children in an institution made the calculations a lot easier. You just divided the costs of running the institutions by the number of children served. Hopefully, you got a number somewhere less than $11 a month.

In the mid-70s World Vision employed a new cadre of development workers. These were professionally trained men and women who worried about things like empowerment and sustainability. Things like measuring change, goal setting, evaluation. A lot of these people seemed to have an inbuilt bias against the child sponsorship scheme.

A battle between fund-raisers and fund-spenders was brewing, and I originally sided with the first camp.

"Why is my job title 'Communications Officer', and not 'Marketing Officer'?"

David Longe, my first boss, lowered his head and looked at me sadly. "Because *marketing* is still a dirty word in World Vision. Too worldly. So, we don't do *marketing*, and we don't do *advertising*. We do *communications*."

"Well, that's silly," I replied. All that experience in MYF rallies and Gold Coast discos, not to mention ten years in commercial radio, gave me a different opinion. David, who had come from the Information Office of the Sydney Anglican church, agreed.

"We need to educate some World Vision people about the real world."

Some education was needed on both sides because I needed to learn how the world of aid and development was changing. And how World Vision was changing with it.

At the heart of our problem was an ethical issue. Does our advertising tell the truth? What do sponsors think? What do we want them to think? As the person responsible for writing our advertising copy, I wanted to write: "Rescue this child!"

The advertising fed on ancient elitist attitudes to the poor: Ideas like welfare as a solution, like rich people giving to the poor is a noble thing, like *we're so rich, we should do something*. Like money is the answer. However, the world of poverty is much more complex, and we were promoting a simple method that obscured the complexity.

At first, we introduced the World Vision Aid Team. For $30 a month, donors funded community development projects. These might involve a World Vision change agent working with the community.

Child Sponsorship Needed Fixing

Help them discover what needed to be done, and in what order. She or he would work with the existing leaders in a community. Do a survey. Ask probing questions. The community might start with something small and simple. Build a cover over the bus stop where the kids wait for the school bus. From little things, bigger things grew.

More projects funded by child sponsors were moving towards this developmental way of working. How to align what was in sponsors minds with on-the-ground reality? One solution was to ensure that every sponsored child received an identifiable benefit. Marketers called this the Minimum Benefits Package. This was not a solution. It was a recognition that something was out of kilter.

"We have a communications problem." Another international meeting in Los Angeles in a sterile, air-controlled room. Jugs of water. Plastic glasses. Yellow notepads. Sharp Ticonderoga HB pencils. A jet-lagged audience. And me, more tired than most after the flight from Hong Kong via Japan.

"Do tell," drolled Chris Radley, the British marketing guru. His tone ironic. I recognised he agreed.

"I've been in World Vision now for seven years. This is the third or fourth time we've talked about child sponsorship and got nowhere." A few heads nodded, some of them into slumber.

"What do you propose, Phil?" The Americans always called me Phil. I didn't mind. I was "Phil" for a decade on radio.

"Have you ever met a single child sponsor who visited their child's project and came away disappointed?"

"No. Once they see what's happening in the project, they're turned on. They love it. They're our best promoters. What do you think? Give every sponsor an air ticket?"

"I wish," I smiled. "We should put together a couple of teams. Marketers and some of our best development minds. We should sit in a project and say, 'How can we communicate the truth of what's happening here?'"

Salvador, Brazil, was our first attempt. We learned a lot. Development workers and marketers together. Teaching each other. How it looks from the donor's point of view. How it looks here on the ground. What do the people think about donors? We sat on the ground, and in the homes of families living in places where World Vision was working. We talked over meals and evening drinks. We met formally with whiteboards and coloured markers. We taught and learned.

After a week, Chris Radley and I spent a day designing an alternative way of communicating the truth of our work. I wrote words. Chris sketched flyers, folders, ads and brochures.

Two weeks later, we flew to Kenya and repeated the exercise. It was a thrilling and motivating experience. There was a lot of enthusiasm. But there was another issue that soon scuttled further progress.

All the support offices jointly funded child sponsorship projects. This would have been fine except that every support office had set the monthly sponsorship rate to suit their own markets. I recall the rates ranging from 10 US dollars to about 30 per month. Exchange rates fluctuated every day. Sponsor's giving the lower rate were effectively being subsidised by the higher donors.

A few of us suggested the solution was simple. Instead of every country having a share in every project, allocate whole projects to each support office. A simple calculation would reveal how many sponsors we needed for each project. More for the lower rate countries; fewer for the higher rates. We called this "project brokering".

Unfortunately, there was little further collaboration. The US office decided unilaterally to go its own way, by altogether abandoning the linkage between child and sponsor and launching a new program called "Childcare Partners." The Americans were admirably, if blindly, committed to their solution and such was the weight of American influence and money, they were not to be turned. Their belief removed commitment to try anything else. Its failure left us with no progress on other ideas, although Britain persisted, and later New Zealand went quietly about their own business.

We almost got back on track when the project brokering idea was later revived. For me, the most important goal in the project brokering idea was achieving a clearer relationship between what sponsors give and what happens in their child's project. In the end, we seemed to have attained all the secondary goals of the project brokering idea without achieving this central one.

More work would wait until the next decade.

* * *

17

Oriental And Lifestyle Questions

Rent was cheap nowhere in Hong Kong. We carried our expectations from Melbourne suburbs and settled well away from Downtown in distant Chek Chue, or Stanley in the colonial language.

"Look first in Mid-Levels," friends advised. "That's where the executives live."

The executive ghettoes were twenty-storey forests of pencil thin apartment blocks stacked up the steep rise above Central, offering spectacular views and chronic vertigo.

Judith decided she preferred to live closer to Mother Earth. I took no convincing. The small community of Stanley, with its fishing village and bus connection to the Star Ferry, looked promising. Stanley contained a fine eponymous French restaurant, a labyrinth of shops selling fake fashion labels, souvenirs and Chinese *bric-à-brac*, a cluster of three-storey apartment blocks, one high-rise and a patrolled swimming beach.

Our third-floor apartment topped out the block which looked over the beach. A screen of she-oaks filtered our view of the road, and the bay beyond. Tai Tam Bay stretched out to the China Sea to our right and directly across to Tai Tam headland, bearing the ugly scar of a disused quarry in its tropical green flanks. A number ten typhoon decapitated the she-oaks halfway through our sojourn, which much improved the view. Small fishing boats bobbed on the morning waters and, in summer, the bay was a panoply of sailboards.

The apartment, unlike more expensive ones closer to Central, was spacious. Three big bedrooms. Two bathrooms. A large central walk-in linen closet. The lounge and dining area was one large open room that extended from the front of the apartment to the back.

Hanging off the dining area was a compact room rather like a mini-flat. Here, crammed in an area not much larger than one of the regular bedrooms, was a maid's room, shower and toilet, laundry and a kitchen. My grandmother was the last person in my family to live in a home with a live-in maid—and she was the maid—so we had no plans to hire an *amah*. Instead, I took over the maid's room as a study for my postgraduate endeavours, and Judy made the neighbouring kitchen and laundry her domain.

Every room had a hole in the wall for an air-conditioner, and we quickly became the owners of six. As winter gave way to summer over the next few months, we delighted in their efficiency.

The plumbing seemed to have a personality. I put this down to the large colony of cockroaches in the drains. Bigger and noisier than Queensland 'roaches, one that flew by Judy was "as big as a bird," she assured me. Her scream of horror as it made its way from bath to window was heard in Australia.

Our neighbours included an airline pilot, a merchant banker, and the landlord who owned a Rolls Royce. The rent was cheaper than Mid-levels, but still more than my entire salary. Since World Vision International was paying most of the rent, I felt well motivated to get the job done, and get out.

Some special foreigners come to live like locals. *Special* is too weak an adjective: they are gifted saints. I had met such worthies. They appeared in every World Vision project I visited. Some were from the community they served. Others were out-of-towners. Some were foreigners. All were living a calling, a vocation. Their commitment to live and work alongside the poor disturbed me. What did I lack that allowed me to settle my family in a spacious three-bedroom apartment, while *real* Christians were sharing a bedroom in Kowloon City or Mong Kok?

Conversations with these immersed missionaries were generous and non-judgemental. While I might have been making judgements about myself, none of them dropped a guilt trip on me.

In time, I found moral peace. The skills required for at-the-coalface living differed from my own. I reasoned that my role was to work hard to make their work possible. I was a fundraiser. My work made their work possible. I knew they appreciated my work in the same way I respected theirs.

We lived a Melbourne-style middle-class lifestyle in Hong Kong, which meant we were among the rich. Our car was a humble Mazda 323, but few people owned cars and many who did had chauffeurs. We did not have a live-in amah or Filipina Maid, although Judy succumbed to peer pressure for a while, engaging a once-a-week woman to do the ironing and cleaning. Judy, in fine Aussie tradition, could not bear to have someone visit, even an employee, unless she first cleaned the flat herself.

The rich/poor gap was a fact of life in Hong Kong, in a way different from Australia. At home, our suburbs form ghettoes of social and economic strata. In Melbourne, rich folk live in Toorak. The working class in Reservoir. The upper middle class in Doncaster. The lower middle class in Boronia.

In Hong Kong everyone lived in sight of everyone else. From Causeway Bay by the Harbour, you could look at the nearby fabulous hotels and shopping centres. Lift your eyes and there were the high-rise apartments, and occasional mansions, of Hong Kong's middle and upper classes. Higher on the hill, the ramshackle sheds of the poor. A socio-economic layered cake.

Much is gone now. When we lived in Stanley there were two distinct communities. Ours was expatriate and wealthy. We clustered in spacious apartments around the beach. Nearby was Stanley shopping village, separated from our posh places by the bus terminal. Beyond the shopping village, creeping up the side of the hills towards a temple, was a village of locals. Their houses were makeshift, unplanned and crowded, but supplied with electricity and other conveniences.

I was there to do a job. That was the easier part. Once I learned the marketing landscape of Hong Kong, it was a matter of putting to work lessons learned Down Under. We quickly gained supporters and, like we had discovered at home, many came from the working class. One category was new—the *nouveau riche*.

In Australia, this socio-economic group was under-represented among our supporters. But in Hong Kong, we found them enthusiastic. They gave from their wealth and wanted to take part.

"My parents came to Hong Kong with nothing," said a supporter who had become a Partner in an accounting firm. He gained his qualifications, and a decent Aussie accent, at Melbourne University. "I remember how hard it was in the old days. We were poor. Now we are not, we have responsibilities." No special convincing, no guilt-inducing advertising, no special appeal beyond the facts of his own life.

As a result, events worked well in Hong Kong. We imported the *40 Hour Famine* but renamed it as the *30 Hour Famine*. China is the home of many superstitions. Language can have good or bad omens. In Chinese, the number four and the word death sound the same.

"You can't call it the forty-hour famine," my communications manager wailed, "we'll DIE!"

We settled for thirty because three and heart sound the same. And my staff assured me that, given the Chinese respect for food, thirty hours would be plenty long enough.

We had been privileged to experience the communications reach of *Neighbours* in Australia. When a character in that TV soap joined the *40 Hour Famine*, participation exploded. In Hong Kong, World Vision was not a household name. Yet, there was one program on the Chinese language TV channel that every Cantonese-speaking family watched every night. Called *Hong Kong Tonight*, it was, like *Neighbours*, set in a typical Hong Kong family. Traditional parents and modern children shared an apartment in the more crowded part of Kowloon.

I watched with delight, and little Cantonese fluency, as one daughter in the family came home with a *30 Hour Famine* sign-up sheet. We enjoyed a deluge of interest in the *30 Hour Famine*. World

Vision was part of the family life of "Hong Kong Tonight" and so it was part of the life of Hong Kong itself. Such is the power of television.

The telephones rang. "I want to be in the *30 Hour Famine*." "Please sign up my whole family." "My school class wants to be in it." And then a chorus of "What else can I do?"

They wanted to *do* things. We saw this at the *30 Hour Famine* live-in camps. Hundreds of young Hong Kong supporters camped overnight with plenty of water to drink, lots of musical entertainment and games. The enthusiasm of the youth of Hong Kong was both naïve and lovely. It was a joyful experience, not least because the World Vision staff carried off the organisation with no real help from me. Forced by my lack of knowledge of how to make things happen, I delegated. I discovered that trust often brings rewards beyond expectations.

During these three-and-a-half years I completed a master's degree in Business Administration with Deakin University. This was "learning by extension" in the academic lingo, but I called it "off-campus". After completing the first year of the four-year part-time degree, I became the test bunny for a truly off-campus experience by continuing my studies in Hong Kong.

Internet and email were still a decade away, although early adopters were firing up Commodore 64s and their many imitations. Large parcels arrived at our Stanley Beach home courtesy of a DHL courier. I returned assignments by the same means. I could borrow references from the library by mailing or faxing requests, and they arrived a few days later from the courier. Even my graduation certificate came by courier. All this was free.

Yes, free. For a moment in time, it was possible to receive an Australian post-graduate education for nothing, save hard work. This was a privilege granted to my generation. Like many of my fellow students, I was the first person in my family to graduate from a University. My father did not, nor his father, nor his grandfather. And his great-grandfather was a convict.

I graduated in 1985 without ever having set foot on the actual campus in Waurn Ponds, near Geelong, Victoria. I sat examinations at the Hong Kong Polytechnic University—me and a single invigilator sharing a large lecture theatre. Face-to-face meetings with my professor happened only when he organised a stopover in Hong Kong *en route* to a family holiday in Britain. We enjoyed a splendid Chinese meal. Perhaps we talked about my studies. I don't think we did.

Combining study with foreign life had its riches. The challenges of culture mapped into the challenges of organisational life. Getting things done in the shops informed how to do things in the accounts department. How to relate to significant people in the outside community informed how to deal with organisation hierarchy. Much of this coalesced into my mini thesis. I wrote on organisational culture: "Organisations Are People Too."

Some people, when gifted with new knowledge, feel obliged to inform the ignorant masses. And that is what I did, but with a twist. When I learned something new, I believed I was just catching up with common knowledge. I thought everyone must know this, and I blundered into conversations without realising if my audience was with me. Either they did not understand and needed to catch up, or what I had just learned really was common knowledge and didn't need saying.

Back in Los Angeles, my boss, Colonel (retired) Hal Barber received a two-page memo from me outlining the cure for a problem at the international office. Hal, with typical grace, sent me a telex:

"Phil, do you have enough to do over there? Hal."

* * *

18

Make Mistakes–
Learn From Them

It was no-one's intention to stay in Hong Kong a long time, but the success of Hong Kong, and then in Singapore, suggested possibilities. Expansion in Europe had begun with a single coordinating office in England. It had spawned offices in Germany, Ireland, Finland and the Netherlands. Hal Barber suggested I might look to Taiwan and Japan. Maybe, if I was brave (or foolhardy) even China.

Despite the attraction of such adventures, a family consideration prevailed. The trump card was Jamie and Melanie's looming teenage years.
    We had met many families whose children seemed to have a sense of Statelessness because they lived their first twenty years of life outside their own culture. This was not invariably a bad thing. Some children developed an ability to be at home anywhere in the world: others seemed never at home wherever they were.

Our choice as parents was roots were important, and we chose Australia for the teenage years. Soon, we wanted to go home.

That meant I had to find a local to lead World Vision Hong Kong.

We advertised. A few responses were worth following up. One stood out. A man in his early thirties, working in an international organisation with a head office in Europe. He was married, with a daughter, and attended church. He was born in Hong Kong, educated locally, spoke Cantonese as his mother tongue, Mandarin adequately, and English well. He was pleasant, dressed well and looked me in the eye. I interviewed him, liked him, and appointed him.

It was a disaster.

I blame myself. Rightly. I had a lot to learn about staff selection. I had not learned about the *Halo Effect*. I was influenced by this man's look, demeanour and job history. This halo of attractive features swayed me to overlook anything else. Truthfully, I asked no questions about how he managed people, how he approached problems, whether he could describe some success in his career he had been proud of, what disappointed him in his previous work and why. I just liked the cut of his jib. I didn't notice that he didn't have a mainsail.

My natural approach in a new job is to listen more than talk. I realised that this approach was only one of many.

"Look for the low hanging fruit," some mentor had told me.

It resonated. Usually, one finds something that everyone in the organisation has been aching to fix. Fix it and you're a hero. The key is to find something that is (a) easy to fix and (b) will make everyone, or almost everyone, happy. It doesn't have to be huge. My first action on becoming CEO of World Vision Australia some years later, was to get the office curtains washed. Others on the 8th floor noticed. It seemed like I was there to clean things up.

"Welcome!" I said on that first morning with my new man. I explained again that he would report to me in my capacity as chair of the board of World Vision Hong Kong, and that, for the next few months at least, I would be in the office every day to assist him. "Take your time. Learn what we do, and you'll soon see what our strengths and weaknesses are."

Within a week, there was quiet uproar. It was a very Chinese response. Inscrutable faces worked with my new man while he talked more than listened and ordered more than learned. Quietly, the office whispered its concerns to my two senior colleagues, Barbara, in charge of Finance and Admin, and Margaret, in charge of Communications and Marketing. Cups of tea were drunk in nearby hotel lobbies. I was gently and firmly given the news.

A week after his arrival, he invited my family to meet his wife and daughter over a meal. By the time the date came around, I knew I would let him go. He was out of his depth. I had hired a clerk when I needed a leader.

Without telling Judy what I had planned for the next day, we took the MTR to Sha Tin, a then burgeoning new town beyond Lion Rock. The evening was congenial. I was in guilty agony with hypocrisy. Superficial cordiality tonight. Tomorrow I will fire you. I grieved for his wife's innocence. I suspected she would hate me tomorrow.

I had never fired anyone. "Never" was merely a few years of management experience. People came and went from my communications team in Australia, but I had never had to manage a dismissal.

The next day in Prat Avenue seemed to be a relief for everyone, the discarded CEO included. My decision surprised him, but he offered no resistance. *Labour laws* was an oxymoron in Hong Kong, but we offered him pay in lieu of notice, and we never heard from him again.

One useful outcome from the saga was the changed relationship between Barbara and Margaret. These two managers were frequently at odds. Managing their relationship was a major part of my job. In my temporary CEO, they had found a common enemy.

"Barbara and I got on much better after that," Margaret confessed soon after. Barbara, sitting beside her in my office, smiled. It was enough.

I took a deep breath and advice from others about job hiring practices. A second round of advertising some months later yielded a successful candidate who fitted the role well. With my CEO now in place, I could implement my exit strategy.

We were in Hong Kong for nearly four years. Judith will always point out it was "exactly three-and-a-half years." It was a shaping experience for us all. Living outside one's own culture leaves you unmoored for a while. Coping requires some selflessness and other-awareness. To succeed in a Chinese culture, I had to learn to let go of many taken-for-granted assumptions about how the world operated.

Like always being called "Mr Hunt". The staff insisting I have an office of my own. It was respect they wanted to give me, and perhaps it was better I was out of their way. Although, all our offices had glass walls. Barbara Tse and Margaret Li, my two key managers, became reliable colleagues, and even though our relationship was friendly, it was unlike the relationship I may have had with an Australian colleague. Our cultural differences made it different.

Everyone should live outside their culture for at least one year. I encourage young people to travel. Stay away for more than a year. You will learn a lot about yourself.

Late in our Hong Kong sojourn we went home to Melbourne for a holiday. I spent two days walking the corridors of my old World Vision Australia haunts. Reflecting on this two-day immersion later, I ventured opinions on management in a memo to my former boss, Harold Henderson. Harold took this with more grace than I deserved but delayed a response until he visited us. Harold generously shared about problems in his family life that were common knowledge in the organisation, and which later would lead to divorce. He proposed to move the family to Sydney. Yet he wanted to continue in his leadership role. I wondered how that could work.

"That memo you wrote me after you visited," Harold said. I remembered suggesting a Chief Operating Officer role like our International Office. I recalled it contained an unveiled hint about who might fill that role. Harold said he would discuss the matter with his Board.

A month or two later we were on the Qantas flight back to Australia. I was to discover that the job I had described *did not exist*.

* * *

Book 4

Displaced At Home

19

Not *That* Job, *This* Job—Maybe I Should Quit

The journey to my Hong Kong office required a bus, a ferry and a brief walk. The number six bus that climbed the mountain behind our flat was invariably crowded and, in summer, an oven. You paid twice the price for the alternative number 260 bus (but still only about $1.50 in Aussie coin). For that you got air-conditioning and speed since it drove through the Aberdeen tunnel, under the mountain. You would rarely find a seat on the Star Ferry, but it was open to the elements. No matter the heat of the day, one could be assured of a breeze.

The walk from the ferry to the office involved crowded footpaths which invited everyone to maintain a walking pace suited to those blessed with a stride shorter than mine. I could see over the passing parade. Spot the occasional moment to stride out.

The city state was in constant motion. Buildings appeared almost daily. The harbour was a heaving maze of craft—tiny dinghies to ocean liners and the occasional Junk. Advertising signs covered every wall of the city. Tiny one room shops proclaimed themselves as "Worldwide Emporiums". Hawkers appealed to get a suit made or buy a "copy-watch". Many of the signs made ludicrous sense to an English-speaking mind. Daily I spotted the sign for "Fuk Hing Furniture" and wondered what that looked like. Once I got over the culture shock of so much activity, noise and movement, these journeys became a daily delight.

Back in Melbourne, I missed their ease. The train journey from Boronia to Flinders Street lacked fresh air and panoramic views. I looked at graffiti instead. The tram to South Melbourne lacked magic. When work provided me a car, I drove to work instead. At least behind the wheel I could be in charge.

Meanwhile, I was struggling to understand what had gone wrong.

In my mind I was coming back to the role of Deputy Chief Executive—a copy of the International office. When the President, Stan Mooneyham, had appointed Hal Barber to be his Executive Vice President, he placed Hal between himself and the next layer of Vice Presidents. There were five or six Vice Presidents—three responsible for World Vision's work in Asia, Africa and Latin America, and others for administrative functions. Doubtless, some of these Vice Presidents weren't thrilled to have an EVP between them and the President, but I thought it was working well.

This structure is not uncommon. A Chief Executive Officer (CEO) mainly having a strategic focus, while a Chief Operating Officer (COO) manages the internal operations. It requires a symbiotic relationship to work well, and it helps if the COO isn't ambitious for the CEO's job. Hal Barber was a man with more than enough achievements in his career already, and his humility in working with Stan and subsequent Presidents, was an impressive model. I took note.

However, Harold explained to me that the Australian Board "did not want to make an appointment that implied succession." I suppose it's to my credit that this surprised me. "Succession" seemed a remote idea. Was I being honest with myself? Did I really have a plan to oust Harold from his job? Was I that ruthless? Did the Board see me that way?

I recalled being offended when my first World Vision boss, David Longe, had said that I had "eyes on his seat". It caused me to examine my heart, and I didn't see my ambition focussed so personally. I didn't want David's seat. I hoped that nothing I did or said ever gave that impression. Would I have liked the chance to do his job? Yes. But so long as David was in the position, the question was hypothetical. I was not thinking about it.

Did I lack ambition? Not at all. As I learned more, I wanted to do more. As I gained experience, I wanted to exercise what I had learned. I was ambitious for opportunities. I would look for those opportunities when they arose. When they were on offer. Harold's position was not within my right to contemplate. I didn't.

Boards may be jealous of their responsibility to hire and fire chief executives. As chair of the fledgling board of World Vision Hong Kong, I had already experienced something of that responsibility. In time, I would revisit it many times. The choice is rarely easy, and the view from the Board is rarely the same as the view of the outgoing CEO. I hadn't considered that the position of deputy might appear to give me a career advantage. Some must have seen it that way.

Boards need to consider the "Peter Principle"—that people rise to their level of incompetence. Maybe the Board wanted a longer look at me, and the other options. All sensible, but I felt let down.

I had burnt bridges. Judy, Jamie and Melanie had grown comfortable in Hong Kong. It wasn't their idea to leave. We left friends behind. Living the expatriate life, far from the rest of our families, had strengthened our family bonds. It would have been easy to stay. But now, a ship steaming towards Melbourne carried a container load of our furniture. Jamie was 13. Melanie 12. Arrangements were in place for them to start school at Kingswood College in Box Hill. Fees had been paid. Judy and I had discussed renovations to our Boronia home. There was no turning back.

I felt powerless to do anything. Why was I hearing this news only *now*? Why did Harold invite me home to be his operational deputy without clearing it with his Board? This seemed careless, at worst it was unjust. I was working for an organisation that believed in social justice. Harold Henderson was an exemplary leader in reminding World Vision that aid without justice is less than half the job. I felt demoted. I had come to lead a team. I expected the authority to do the job. The taste of leadership from Hong Kong remained. This new flavour had a bitter edge.

While I felt a slap in my ambitious face, I doubted there was anyone wanting to hear my tiny violin. And seriously, why complain? I had talented friends to work with. My role in coordinating operations was clear, even if my authority might be sometimes vague. It relieved my new colleagues that their own reporting relationships had not altered. I determined to make the best of it. It was the right course. I learned a lot about how to get things done when you have little power.

It was enough to be back in Australia with a fresh challenge. Call me stupid, but I didn't assume that the new position would be a steppingstone to CEO. I didn't have a long-term career plan. Bank Johnny, to radio announcer, to journalism student, to copywriter, to communications director, to manager of a start-up. It had a certain logic, but only in retrospect. Had I been able to forecast where the next two decades might take me, I would have been even more surprised.

I became Director of Strategic Planning and Executive Team Leader, a job title both wordy and vague. Like other members, I reported to Harold. No-one reported to me. Among the Executive Team, I was to be *primus inter pares*. First Among Equals. I soon learned it was an oxymoron. In any language.

* * *

20

Stress Can Make You Sick

Wheels turning. Huge, heavy wheels. Grinding like huge cogs with wide teeth, silently. Quiet pressure. Intense, thick pressure. Inside. Behind my eyes. And higher. Pushing. Gripping.

"You're just having a nightmare, Philip."

I'm on Gran's lap. She's not a tall woman, but there's plenty of her. And she's soft. Just what a child with a migraine needs. A place to rest his head.

"Big wheels, turning."

"There, there. It'll go away soon."

She's right. It goes away. I sleep again. Until next time.

Mum carried a small box of powders in her handbag. From the box she would extract a flat paper packet. It reminded me of great-grandfather's Tally-ho cigarette papers, but larger. Great-grandfather Pegler needed to fill his papers with tobacco, Mum's came pre-filled with pink powder.

Vincent's APC. She took it for headaches. Some of those headaches put her in bed for the day. I should have seen the link.

APC stood for aspirin-phenacetin-caffeine. Phenacetin was later banned, because it can kill you. Ask Howard Hughes, whose kidneys didn't survive a lifetime of painkillers. Emphasis on *killers*.

Truth is, Vincent's, and its soulmate, Bex, did nothing for migraines. Promoted as mothers' little helper with the slogan, "a cup of tea, a Bex and a good lie down", only the lie down was useful for migraine. Lie down in a quiet dark room until it passed.

Mum and I were among the luckier afflicted. Migraine attacks were intermittent. Most days were fine. The heavier clouds appeared in clusters about monthly and a good lie down was the best medicine, leaving us woozy and brain-slow for the rest of the day.

I discern all this in retrospect. I'm not sure Mum ever labelled her headaches and periods of disappearance as migraine. I don't recall hearing the word until I was about 16, when I had a frightening experience of partial blindness.

Chermside Methodist Church didn't have a Sunday School. Instead, expressing its progressiveness, we had an All-Age Church School. Parishioners of all ages met at nine on Sunday morning. The kiddies out the back spread across the church halls, the adults in the worship centre, and the teens up the road in the rumpus room of the Wayper's house. After an hour of schooling, these disparate groups combined for 10:30 worship. It worked well for a time. It was the structure that later brought Judy and I back into church life after a time in a spiritual desert.

But when I was 16, it became known I could play piano. It became my job to tinkle the ivories on Wayper's piano. One morning as we walked up Hamilton Road, something shimmered in my sight. It was a vee-shaped swirl of nothing, right in the centre of where I was looking. As it grew and moved, I realised I could see nothing around its shimmering. It wasn't blocking my sight. It was erasing it. I had a distinct blind spot exactly where I wanted to look.

My peripheral vision seemed OK, so I could continue to walk and talk, although I said nothing to others as we trudged up the hill. And then slowly, in the fifteen minutes it took to arrive and get started, the shimmering caret and its accompanying blind spot moved from the centre of my vision. Finally, it drifted off somewhere to the top right of my visual world.

Five minutes later. Wheels. Huge, heavy wheels. And piano playing in a fog. At times like these, and there would be others, muscle memory guides the fingers.

Frightened that I was about to go blind, I related the experience to Mum and Dad. Dr Anderson, our friendly GP, diagnosed migraine. My blind spot experience was not a sign of impending blindness, but a symptom of migraine.

There is a connection between stress and migraine. At least for me. And there is a connection between structure and stress. I was about to endure it in my new role as *first among equals*.

* * *

21

Primal Scream Therapy

Harold moved to Sydney. The rest of his executive team remained in 161 Sturt Street, South Melbourne. His team comprised Communications Director (Dave Toycen), Finance and Administration Director (Kevin Gray), Donor Services Director (Bert O'Brien), and Human Resources Manager (Merilyn Hill). Yes, that the only woman on the team wore the title *Manager* went unobserved.

Kevin, Bert and Merilyn had been colleagues before. We had recruited Dave to fill my Communications Director position. They were a good bunch. Well experienced. I had known them all for years. Full of MBA hubris, I tried to move things around. It wasn't easy.

There are two kinds of authority. Positional and Personal. You have authority based on your position, and that depends a lot on who is your boss. Everyone on this team had similar positional authority— we all reported to Harold. Some incumbents think their position is more important than others, which is why accountants, marketers and engineers jostle. Effective leaders can harness that difference, or it can descend into unproductive conflict.

Personal authority comes from knowledge and experience. Dave and I had our international experiences that carried some weight. Merilyn and Kevin had more years of service with World Vision than the rest. Bert had moved from leading the representative team to managing donor services, which gave him a wide experience across the organisation. We were a pretty even bunch.

So, how to lead? If I had a plan, it was to cross each bridge as it came. World Vision itself taught this in Effective Community Development 101. It also works for Organisational Development. Do Step One. Evaluate. Redesign Step Two in the light of your evaluation. Do Step Two. Repeat.

Inch by Inch anything's a cinch.–John Bytheway.

Since Harold managed remotely in faraway Sydney, I proposed two regular meetings. When the boss wasn't in town, I would chair a meeting to deal with operational issues that didn't require reference to the boss. I called this the *Executive Team Meeting*, or ETM. It met weekly for about two hours. We decided by a rough consensus, or we deferred to Harold's next appearance.

When the boss was in town, which was at least twice a month for a few days at a time, we would meet as the *Executive Strategy Team*. This became known as the ESM. Our agenda then was the things we had found impossible to decide without Harold's right of veto.

Did it work? Yes, more or less.

Was it easy? Not for me. Consensus leadership is fine for maintaining the status quo, but if I wanted innovation, these things needed the CEO imprimatur. I often felt that ETMs without Harold were just going through the motions. Wading in molasses. I'm sure others in the team felt the same, but we kept the ship of World Vision on an even keel.

It was during this time that I invented Primal Scream Therapy. My version of this was first exhibited *en route* to a day in the office that I knew would require patience, sensitivity and political smarts. Some days as I got closer to the office I was in an emotional turmoil of dread

Primal Scream Therapy

and anxiety. There was a moment, while I waited for traffic congestion to spew me onto the Monash Freeway, when I wound up the car radio and screamed. Loudly. Full decibels.

Very liberating. I recommend it. But keep the windows closed.

Fortunately, World Vision Australia was about to have its most successful fundraising year ever, riding the *Feed the World* wave. Nothing like kicking goals to keep the team happy.

* * *

22

When Life Serves Up Lemons, Make Lemonade

The first year after we returned from Hong Kong, World Vision Australia's income grew 150%. It was a credit to the strength of our marketing team, and the efficient administrative follow-up—but also because of an Irish rock star.

Bob Geldof, singer-songwriter from the *Boomtown Rats*, had seen a BBC News report on "a famine of Biblical proportions" by Michael Buerk. He described scenes of starvation in Ethiopia as "Hell on Earth." The brief report was shown around the world. Geldof's response was to form *Band Aid*, a charity supergroup to raise money to fight the famine. In 1984, *Band Aid* released a single, "Do They Know It's Christmas?" and it became an instant hit, selling over a million copies in the first week.

Starvation in Ethiopia may have been news to the world, but to the many aid groups battling daily in Ethiopia, it was familiar. In 1983, Anne Deveson had accompanied Ossie Emery and me to a similar scene of wretchedness in Northern Ethiopia. Our report had made some impact in Australia, but when the BBC report connected with Bob Geldof's activism, the story went world-wide.

The situation in Ethiopia since 1983 had become increasingly deadly. All the agencies working there were short of resources, and desperate to get the world's attention. Jacob Akol, a British-educated Sudanese, was working as a media officer for World Vision. In a fortuitous encounter, he persuaded Michael Buerk that there was a story in Ethiopia. Jacob offered to help.

Band Aid and its *Feed the World* campaign was an instant success. Geldof had modest ambitions for the campaign, predicting it might raise about £70,000. Those of us familiar with fundraising might have advised him to be bolder. The total was over £8 million!

On 14th July 1985, I was in a motel in Kew, fresh off the plane from Hong Kong and waiting to get back into our Melbourne home. I was ready to plunge into my new role as the *first among equals*. Across the world, including in Kew, we switched our television sets to *Live Aid*. It was the biggest television broadcast ever. Two concerts—one in London, the other in Philadelphia—were seen around the world. Ethiopian famine was seen in every lounge room.

For organisations like World Vision, the result proved the value of free publicity. Income was up 150% and the *40 Hour Famine* had its best result ever.

Being *first among equals* wasn't all I had to do. I remained chair of the Board of World Vision Hong Kong for the next few years. Likewise, although we had no official Board in Singapore, I met there regularly with CEO, Goh Eng Kee, and key supporters within the Singapore Government. The Hong Kong board dealt with leadership changes, including a CEO who faced a sexual abuse charge. I was impressed with the quality of people we recruited to that Board. In particular, I was impressed with Dr. Daniel Tse Chi-wai, LLD, GBS, CBE, JP, who was President of the Hong Kong Baptist College (and later University) and who succeeded me as chair. Daniel guided us through the difficulties with a steady, firm hand.

The Singapore situation was unique. Friendly relationships with the Administration were essential, subtle and private. World Vision was the only international aid organisation permitted to have a local

When Life Serves Up Lemons, Make Lemonade

fundraising office. I am sure the relationships were key to its success.

Harold continued to be generous in inviting me to take part in the international arena. Sometimes I deputised for him in International Meetings.

When I joined World Vision in 1976, I knew everyone in the Australian office by name. This was no monumental feat. We were about 80 people, spread across the 11th and 12th floors of a narrow corner of Elizabeth and Little Collins Streets, Melbourne. I have a photo of the entire staff assembled on the rooftop fire escape. I'm near the top, being a larrikin.

Ten years later there were twice as many people. We spread over four floors of a building at 161 Sturt Street, South Melbourne. I would ride the lift to my 8th floor workstation and frequently encounter a new face *en route*.

"Hi, I'm Philip."
"Yes, I know. I'm Kathy."
"Where do you work, Kathy?"
"Here. World Vision."
"Oh yes. I mean, which department?"
"In the phone room, with Malcolm Winton."
"Great. Well, welcome to World Vision."
"I'm not new. I've been here three years."

Obviously, I needed to get out more. But also, we needed more activities that enabled the people of the organisation to move outside their own rooms. Groups formed to work on the once-a-week staff meeting. We informally called it "Big Devos" to contrast it with the morning devotions that occurred in some departments. Big Devos was a combination of worship music, prayer, news, announcements, humour and, usually, a guest speaker. It ran for an hour, usually first thing on Wednesdays. Not everyone wanted to attend, so we made it valuable and used the office rumour mill to deliver the hint we wanted everyone there.

Once a year, we would shut the office down for a day and just have fun together. Some wanted to make it a "Day of Prayer" as was the tradition in the American office. Nothing wrong with that, but I encouraged the organising group to add in some fun and nonsense, to throw us together in new configurations. It might be the only time you would get to meet Kathy outside of the lifts.

When I look at my diaries of this time, I see there are task forces, committees and review groups meeting two or three times a week. Most of them I got started or gave them an occasional push. This was one more way that people could interact in unfamiliar ways. Not only that, but they also produced improvements, and a group of champions to push change ahead.

* * *

23

Challenge The Taken-for-granted Assumptions

It was 29th January in Perth. At Cape Kennedy, where the Challenger space mission was launching, it was the 28th. We remember dates this way. The day the Challenger exploded in a broken spiral of smoke, killing all on board. Including that teacher from Concord, New Hampshire.

The television was on in my hotel room in Perth. The sun had been up a while because it was Summer Down Under. The Bylaws Revision Committee would meet at 9. I had time to watch the launch. And the disaster.

This was my tenth year with World Vision. Starting the day with disaster wasn't a novel experience. The difference was merely that daily disasters like famine, grinding poverty and child malnutrition were unexceptional. Common events are not newsworthy. Only the unusual makes the news, or registers in memory.

At 9 we gathered in the conference room. Rev Dr Noel Vose was chairing the committee and since he lived in Perth, he had chosen the world's most remote State Capital for our first meeting. We had all seen or heard the news of Challenger's demise. Noel prayed. For NASA? I don't remember, but probably. I know he prayed that our work as a committee might be productive. There was some doubt.

A decade earlier, World Vision had launched a bold experiment. It moved from its American roots to become an international organisation. Tom Houston was the President of the international organisation in 1986, and he had seen the bylaws.

"What is good for 1970 may not be good for 1990," Tom suggested to a meeting of his Board. He was echoing the words of Stan Mooneyham to the first meeting of the International Board in 1976. I doubt the echo was unwitting.

A Committee was thus created. Someone asked me to staff it. Our task was to look at the rules governing the organisation, consult widely, and recommend worthwhile changes. The group that assembled that day in Perth were well qualified for the task.

Noel Vose came via the Australian Board. Under Noel's disciplining gaze that day were:

John Allwood, CEO of World Vision South Africa;
David Andrus, Board member of World Vision Canada;
James Mageria, Vice President for Africa;
Harold Henderson, CEO of World Vision Australia;
John Rymer, Board member of World Vision New Zealand, *and me.*

Some months earlier, the committee asked me to explore expectations. I began at the international office. For two weeks I moved from open-plan cubby to cubby, our conversations silenced by the white noise pumped in alongside the air-conditioning. Everyone was frank. Many were earnest. All had opinions. There was little common ground.

"Where you stand depends on where you sit," said someone, sometime. My conversations revealed the truth of it.

The work took many meetings, a million faxes (no email yet), and a lot of words—written and spoken. Together with Janis Balda, a lawyer in the international office, we shouldered most of the secretarial work, sandwiched in between our proper jobs.

The work of the committee narrowed down to what might be

Challenge The Taken-for-granted Assumptions

achievable in the short term, adjusting the balance between sending and receiving offices or, in the language of World Vision, support and field.

From 1976 to 1986, World Vision International's structure was like this:

An International Council which met once every three years, made up of:
- 46 members of the Boards of World Vision Support offices in the USA, Canada, Australia, New Zealand, Germany and Europe. There was a voting system that restricted these 46 persons to 30 votes in total.
- The International President and the nine Vice-Presidents reporting to him.
- The six CEOs of the Support Offices (called Vice-Presidents by virtue of their office).
- Five persons from the Boards of Field Offices in the Asia Region.
- One person from Africa (South Africa, which was a small Support office).
- Nine invited persons described as "members-at-large". Four were from Asia, three from Africa and one each from Latin America and Europe. Some of these members-at-large were CEOs of Field Offices.

76 people. It cost a packet to bring these people together every three years, but such an arrangement was not unusual. The problem the committee faced was changing the balance between support and field. About 90% of the Council was from the West; 10% from the South (or, as the language of the 80s defined, "The Third World").

We proposed:
- 3 members of the Boards of World Vision Support offices in the USA, Canada, Australia, New Zealand, Germany, Britain and Hong Kong (The Europe office to be dissolved).
- The International President and the nine Vice-Presidents reporting to him (or maybe her?).

- Nine Board or Advisory Council members from each of the Asia, Africa and Latin America regions.
- Three CEOs from each of the Asia, Africa and Latin America regions.
- A new category of developing support offices which, in 1986, included one board or staff member from the Support Office Board of South Africa.

68 people. For the time being this gave some capacity to grow with support offices in Ireland, the Netherlands, Switzerland and Austria developing. Fundraising had begun also in Japan. Taiwan, which was a field office, was also raising support much like Hong Kong.

The balance here was about 50:50. It pleased the WVI Council to agree because we had made sure of it well in advance. The committee worked hard, keeping key Council members informed, listening to their concerns and proposing solutions.

It was pleasing to achieve a good outcome. I want to say I learned a lot about the lobbying process. How to do it. When to do it. Why to do it. With whom to do it. But I would later pay a price for not having learned well enough.

In the meantime, there was more than enough stressful work to occupy my mind in Australia. I just needed to work out how to lead.

* * *

24

Leaders, I've Had A Few

I guess someone was in charge of the National Bank when I worked there, but I only knew managers that I reported to. These were leaders well down the line, but from all of them there was something to learn.

Yet, it was only when I fell into my first radio job that I got to see someone who had responsibility for the whole shebang. Pat Maher was the first of these at 4NA Nambour and, as I reported, my strongest memory of him is hardly the kindest. Demonstrative discipline seemed to be his shtick, although if I scratch my fairness bone, only this one encounter has stuck in memory.

Colin Barrett, at 4CA Cairns, I admired as a coach. He was fair, and I wanted to please him.

Robert Walker at 4BK was more remote and shielded by a martinet of a secretary who often conveyed edicts from the front office with clarity and no-correspondence-will-be-entered-into firmness. Her appearance, as she strode straight-backed and tall down the station hallway, never failed to chill.

Meanwhile, Lew Born was a model of a different colour. In some respects, rather like David Longe, he was entrepreneurial and enthusiastic. Uniquely, Lew's enthusiasm was wildly infectious. We borrowed his desires to get things done.

Some leaders follow an inch-by-inch-anything's-a-cinch creed. They inspire by their logical approach. Lew's method sparked ideas from those who caught the infection. Many years later, I would still reflect on how easy it was to get something done when everyone wanted it done. And how hard it was when no-one cared.

As the planets aligned, Lew and I intersected after I had left Methodist youth work behind. When the World Vision Australia Board was looking for a Queensland-based member, Harold Henderson asked me to approach Lew. Lew was enthusiastic. He joined the Board while I was Communications Director and remained through my later stints.

Even more surprising, he later became my pastor. Lew decided he would like another stint at parish ministry. Exhibiting his iconoclastic preferences, he did not choose a Uniting Church parish. Lew accepted an invitation as Senior Minister at Doncaster Church of Christ in Melbourne.

The Sunday after we returned to Australia was Lew's induction at the Doncaster Church. We attended as a one-off. We stayed longer, renewing the benefit of Lew and Betty Born's ministry and friendship, and discovering new long-term friends within that church community.

Harold Henderson was known as Mr Henderson by all the staff, save for a few direct reports. He was a tall, impressive figure, with a gentle manner, but not afraid of delivering a challenge. Towards the end of one frustrating budgeting cycle, our predicted income looked well short of his hopes. Harold invented the "Miracle Million" by adding $1,000,000 to the income line and challenging us to deliver. It worked.

Harold often seemed weighed down by family issues. He kept these mostly to himself, but he was often tired. Many of us learned to avoid long discussions with him in the early afternoon. Harold's marriage finally collapsed into separation and divorce.

I was not alone in believing Harold would have made a quality

World Vision International President. He had a keen political sense, having worked on campaigns with Rev Alan Walker at Wesley Mission, Sydney. Divorce, in World Vision's international world, was anathema to promotion. Harold would never be President.

World Vision International had not enjoyed the best luck with its early Presidents. As a latecomer, I heard the stories of Bob Pierce, World Vision's founder, being painfully shuffled out of the organisation. The rumour was that Stan Mooneyham came under pressure from his Board once his own marriage fell apart. Harold's divorce was a barrier to his advancement owing to the conservativism of the international Board.

Stan left while I was in my first year in Hong Kong and Ted Engstrom assumed the Presidency as a self-proclaimed interim. Everyone seemed to love Ted. I found no reason to demur from the collective opinion. He could make hilarious speeches about World Vision's history, and was a methodical manager-by-objectives, bringing discipline in place of shambles.

I reported to a military man during my time in Hong Kong. Colonel Hal Barber III had served meritoriously in the Berlin Occupation after the Second World War. Hal was a leader of men, a man's man, a military man, but he was no military stereotype. As a foil for Stan, Hal was perfect. Disciplined, unassuming, a servant to the organisation who spoke words of wisdom with charming clarity that encouraged a conversation but never an argument. Firm and fair. I really liked and admired him for his skill, and for never relying on his impressive reputation and life history. Since he never insisted on respect, it was easy to give it.

* * *

25

Learn From Those Who Have Walked The Talk

My role as *first among equals* of the executive team was less than two years old when it became a daily slog. The organisation was bubbling along fine. It continued to grow fast. Income was up every year. Staff were being added. Someone else may have delighted in the familiarity of routine. It bored me. Worse, I was disappointed about myself.

The executive team wasn't really a team. At least, not the team I had imagined we might become. It was not as if team meetings were violent. There was no shouting. Nobody stormed out of meetings. Everyone was polite or, at worst, sarcastic. The meetings were rather *blah*. What was going wrong?

Around this time, I had an epiphany. I discovered the difference between management and leadership. This discovery is not unique to me. It is a rite of passage for a legion of men and women who move into areas of greater responsibility as they learn and grow. But the commonness of the discovery does not limit its significance. It was like a new door opened. The breeze was fresh and full of possibilities.

At an Institute of Management Forum, I heard CEOs talk about their work. Hearing made the difference. I had read most of this stuff before at Uni, but when four chief executives of Melbourne organisations talked, I listened with fresh ears. I learned. Robert Nordlinger was Chair of the TAB; Brian Finn, Managing Director of IBM Australia (I could see his office from my workstation); James Strong, General Manager of Australian Airlines (and soon to be CEO of Qantas); and Mel Ward, Managing Director of Telecom Australia.

They spoke on different topics, yet they were all distinct characters. None of them was charismatic in the Mooneyham sense. Nordlinger came across as tough and opinionated; Finn as people-oriented, primarily a manager of human resources, rather than capital and systems; Strong presented as logical and sincere; Ward as analytical and cerebral. None of them made a brilliant speech. All of them made articulate presentations with sufficient warmth and sincerity to be believable. But all of them left me in no doubt about where they wanted their organizations to go, or what they wanted them to be.

And this, for me in that moment, was the key to leadership. Their job was to articulate the vision.

In these billion-dollar organisations the CEOs did very little else. They articulated the vision by:

1. **People selection.** They removed people who could not accept the vision. Brian Finn said, "You can't sign up for two out of three of IBM's core values. You're committed or you're out."
They installed people from outside who accepted the vision. This seemed to be Nordlinger's key method for getting the TAB in shape. He didn't rely on retraining or brainwashing the existing senior management. He just replaced a lot of them.

2. **Work priorities.** Finn said he made two or three people decisions each week. Decisions to move someone into more or less responsibility; to get someone trained; to give someone recognition. He said he only made two or three financial decisions a year.

Strong saw it as his personal responsibility to spend six weeks doing very little else than travelling around Australia meeting all his staff to explain his vision for Australian Airlines. He planned to do this at least once a year (although he had already done it twice since announcing the change of name from TAA to Australian Airlines 12 months earlier).

Finn involved himself in hundreds of activities at IBM designed to communicate strategic direction. He wrote, and reviewed quarterly with his senior executives, an "elevator speech" which he expected the whole senior team to use. This meant that, if you got into the lift with a senior IBMer and asked, "How's it going?", you got a consistent, simple message about where IBM is heading and what its strategic priorities were. No-one delivered this elevator speech like an automaton. But it meant that even casual conversation focused on reinforcing the firm's direction.

Mel Ward introduced Telecom's Cultural Change Consultant, Greg Campbell. "There are three essential ingredients in changing an organisation," Greg said.

"First, leadership. And you can measure the effectiveness of leadership simply."

Really? I always thought leadership would be a bit soft to measure, but Greg said he could measure it "by the ability of everyone in the organisation to articulate the vision." In that moment, I said to myself, "We would not pass this test."

"Second, education. The most effective is a residential experience that's a couple of weeks long. Definitely not shorter than four days. It has to be intensive, interactive and experiential." I wrote these adjectives down alongside *residential*. But Greg wasn't finished.

"And then, follow up with repeated intervention programs. No further apart than every six weeks. And not less than an entire day."

"Third, mediation." By this, Greg meant all the dozens of ways you could find to communicate the vision and values of the organisation. "And it should focus only on the positive. You only mention the negative to discuss some learning from it."

At this point I raised a tentative hand. "It sounds like propaganda," I said, not too loudly.

"It *is* propaganda," Greg enthused, "but *good* propaganda."

As I drove through the stop-start traffic up Toorak Road to the Eastern Suburbs, through the choked Hartwell intersection where trams and cars jostled for space, I worried how I could even begin to discuss Vision and Values in our organisation. Did we even have a vision?

* * *

26

When Change Is Too Slow, Change Things Slowly

My car was an all-white Holden. It was one of the motoring fashions of the day. A chrome-free Commodore. The front grill was white. The side mirrors were white. I thought it was cool. And I liked to be different. It was indulgent, for sure, but no-chrome was the same price as chrome. The car also had four-on-the-floor and no power steering. A proper bogan car being driven to work by a bearded mid-30s bloke in a suit and tie.

I disliked the idea that you could judge a book by its cover. We always make assumptions about people from how they look, or where they live, or what their job is. I recognised that I did this as much as any person, and I tried to puncture stereotypical assumptions people might have about me. Beards weren't fashionable in the 1980s. I had a "Ned Kelly". The stereotypical senior person at a Christian organisation was short-back-and-sides in a grey suit. I wore sports jackets (how daring, eh?) but permitted a colourful necktie. Later I put my hair in a pony-tail.

But I was neither a radical nor a weirdo. We lived, by preference, in an unexceptional triple-fronted brick-veneer Mission-Brown house in a working-class suburb. We watched *Neighbours* and *Hey, Hey, It's Saturday*. The kids had gone to the State School round the corner. Judy and I were products of middle-class 1950s families. We were imbued with middle-class values. I did not aspire to be Lord of any manor, but I liked to see results from my work. If they offered me more responsibility, I would be offended if someone suggested ambition. I didn't see myself in that way. I would be lying to say I didn't enjoy the recognition or the pay packet. I did. But I never felt it was much of a motivation.

The experience as Executive Team Leader was sobering and disappointing. I wondered if I had leadership qualities. Maybe I was better as a middle manager, moving the deck chairs around to produce more efficiency, challenging people to improve systems. In my heart, I wanted more than this. In my head, I wondered if I had it in me. My personal appraisal suggested the achievements of these past couple of years were on the peripheral, or less crucial areas of my responsibility.

Kevin Gray, my Finance and Admin colleague commented kindly that I had "introduced new discipline to the planning, budgeting and management review processes." I found this a little hard to judge because I felt we still had so much to do before these processes were working satisfactorily.

On the back of explosive income growth in the *Feed-the-World* year, we were now facing a revenue shortfall. Perhaps an improvement on the previous year's phenomenon, but already much less than we had hoped and planned for. I had worked with the team on preparing a revised budget for the second half of the year. The team agreed lower revenue totals and identified areas in which we could reduce spending. Slowing something down, or not doing it at all. We agreed on no staff hires until year end. The result looked promising.

It wasn't.

Year-end figures showed some of our major revenue predictions were good. We had a lot of experience with the larger programs so Child Sponsorship income was on track and the *40 Hour Famine* was healthy. But a half dozen smaller revenue streams had variances of over 10%. In one area we had spent no effort, and yet a $100,000 came in during the second half of the year.

When Change Is Too Slow, Change Things Slowly

Spending bore no relation to prediction. Together we pored over the figures with dismay. We were certain to experience the first year of negative income growth since World Vision began fundraising in Australia.

"There are 27 expense lines over or under budget by more than 10%," gloomed our Finance colleague, Kevin.

"Under is good," I may have suggested. The surrounding faces did not brighten.

"*40 Hour Famine* expenses are 15% over budget," observed Communications Exec, Dave. "That's nearly $200,000. I thought we had a better handle on it than that."

It mystified the team. I knew everyone had taken seriously our intended lowered expectations. None of us had been slack in communicating restraint to our colleagues, but the truth was none of us had the information we needed to do that job.

The One Year Operating Plan showed that too few managers prepared their own plans and budgets. They received the numbers as if from on high. Consequently, there was often no commitment to the result.

One manager was frank. "If you'd asked me in the first place, I would've said this wouldn't work," she said. I wondered *why we didn't ask her in the first place.*

Kevin was right that I had influenced the creation of some new systems, including a purchase order system that included timely reporting to managers of performance against budget at the time of purchase. I wanted managers to have accounting information that aligned with their responsibility. We had made some good starts in this area.

During the next planning cycle we did something new. We delegated control from the half dozen executives, to a further thirty managers. It worked beyond my wildest expectations. Within a year, very few variances set the 10% alarms off. With ownership of their plans, ownership of the results followed.

I was pleased, but strategic planning remained disorganised and unfocused. I felt it was my fault it remained so.

At the same time, we had been experimenting with a sub-branch in Western Australia. Each State had a World Vision office, usually with staff to answer questions and take speaking engagements at schools or churches. I wanted to see if throwing a few more resources to the Perth office could grow support. More donors. More dollars. Harold had been on side, and the Board affirming, but I sensed some colleagues were less enthusiastic. This extra delegation came with some loss of control and authority in communications and donor support areas. No manager enjoys giving power away.

Merilyn Hill was in charge of the Human Resources Department, which had a mostly administrative remit. She had accepted my urging that her department should have a role in staff training and development without giving me the impression she could rise to the task. I shared this impression with her in a frank discussion. I remember we were in my car, returning from lunch in which I had probably said something as encouraging as "I don't think you can deliver what I need." Merilyn had been silent right up to the moment I parked in the downstairs garage.

"You gave Kevin the chance," she said. I didn't know what she meant.

"You wanted changes to accounting, and you gave Kevin the chance to show he could do it. Why would you not give me the chance to prove I can do what you're asking?"

This was fair comment, but it was gutsy. I think I was more impressed by Merilyn's chutzpah in that moment than in my assessment of her capability.

"I think that's fair," I replied. "Let's give it a year and see how you go." Merilyn remained our Human Resources Manager beyond the time I departed. She achieved things by a method I espoused, building a team who could do the things she was not so good at. I always needed HR people, because it wasn't my strength. I always needed Finance people for the same reason.

Merilyn and her team accepted these new directions and worked well in reshaping themselves. But I saw only glimmers that line managers were being held accountable for the development of their own people. Getting a move on training had been a frustrating and demotivating experience for HR and me, and none of the executives seemed to have made training a priority. One or two managers, while taking their own responsibility for staff development seriously, did not link this responsibility into the corporate staff development function.

Staff was trained only within narrow departmental boundaries. Corporate values and objectives were missing. We had an organisation of silos.

I felt a failure most when I considered my own team—the executive team. As a team, it didn't exist.

Back in June 1986 I wrote up, and shared with the other members of the then executive team, my "vision" for the team:

It would be a place in which there was a sense of joint responsibility for World Vision; in which we would balance each executive's "I am" with "We are"; in which our people would hear the word "we" more than the words "you" or the defensive "they".

It would be a group in which relationships were authentic, without artifice or defensiveness; in which the team members would often ask "What do you reckon?" and in return receive honesty without hurt.

Such a group would meet daily. Not because we had an agenda, but because each member wanted to be with the others:

- to share or discover "what's happening".
- to share in the excitement.
- to keep each other "up".
- to enjoy the "other's" goals/achievements.

We would define responsibility by task (Dave on television production, Bert on computers), and the team would define its leadership by the task before it, rather than by job description or position. If you sat in such a team, it might be hard to tell who was the formal leader.

Joint responsibility of such a group would mean:

- earnestly wanting to know what others were doing: but confidently trusting them to do.
- being accountable to the group.
- and, expecting it to hold me accountable.

There was a good practical reason for the executives to work as a team. I was not making a judgment on the way Harold had led the organisation; I was reacting to the increasing challenges of managing an organisation that had doubled in size in less than a decade. It would double again before I left. In Hong Kong I had managed much like Harold had taught me. As Hong Kong CEO, I could get a handle on most of what was going on. We were a staff of three in the beginning. Everyone knew everything. When I left, we were still fewer than twenty.

But now, World Vision Australia had more than a hundred staff. It would grow to nearly 400 by the time I moved on. Decisions could no longer reside in a single chief executive. We needed a new style of leadership.

We were not alone. Soon my favourite football club would move away from a single team captain to a "leadership group". On the field, a group of senior, more experienced players led the team. Off the field, a team of coaches, trainers and assistants led the training. Complexity required new leadership models.

I shared this with the rest of the team in a carefully crafted paper. Their reactions varied from politeness to disagreement.

I failed to communicate what I had in mind, and I was very disappointed. Surely, I thought, everyone will see the plain and obvious logic of my proposal. My method was faulty, of course. No perfectly polished paper ever persuaded. I needed to learn how to give my ideas away, so that others found them and took them as their own. I should have started a discussion and let it build into a group commitment. I had much yet to learn.

In truth, we were not a team.

We met infrequently because we needed a two-hour time slot to share the reports, discuss finances and debate policy changes. By mid-1987 my diary showed we met almost once a week, but the reality was less satisfactory. We met in bursts within a fortnight span, and with one or more of the team members missing or being substituted by a colleague.

It surprised me to discover that the executive group had met as *frequently* as this. My feeling was that it met much less often. I yearned for greater teamwork. Since I was unsatisfied with the quality of teamwork, I probably also felt dissatisfaction at its *quantity*.

We operated in much the same way as under Harold's leadership, except that now there was no true focus for decision making. Since the group wouldn't or couldn't make decisions jointly, sticky problems simmered on the back burners.

I realised I had instinctively come to behave as if I were Deputy Chief Executive. I was sucked into old habits. The team would become a sounding board, and I tried to take the decision myself.

This was unworkable because, despite what Harold had said in the past about the team reporting to me for operational matters, my colleagues had an inconsistent commitment to accepting my authority in this way. I believed there were three reasons for this inconsistency. My title, my own inconsistent behaviour, and the difficulty we had in working out the difference between *strategic* and *operational*.

There were no activities that helped the team to work like a team. I thought we should discuss our values together. Find the common ground. Just after Easter, meeting off-site, I asked the team to discuss "What Easter meant for you?" One colleague told me the discussion was a waste of time. I felt the concept of sharing our values was essential, but I needed to find ways that connected our values to our actual day-to-day work. If I could make that connection, only then would the exercise have value for the team.

In the existing culture, we reported problems up the hierarchy until they reached a common reporting level. Instead of people accepting the work of sorting out problems directly, they complained to their manager. And up the organisational chart the problem went until a common manager resolved the matter. People *said* they had tried to sort out the problem within their departments, but a little probing revealed profoundly different perceptions on what had really happened.

I saw this regularly. Three members of the team routinely came with problems for me to *fix* rather than to the team for resolution. I then made things worse by being too weak to resist. Usually, I followed the cultural pattern and allowed their problem to become my problem. In a team based culture we would keep responsibility for the problem on the managers and have the team meet to help them resolve it. I was allowing managers to delegate upwards those problems which they could resolve through more effective teamwork.

* * *

27

Values And Beliefs Matter

Three influences were coalescing into a strategy.

First, my experience of postgraduate study. In the *amah*'s room, a hot and sweaty offshoot of the inadequately air-conditioned kitchen of our Hong Kong flat, I toiled the Masters in Business Administration to completion. Part of the assessment involved a mini thesis. I titled my project "Organisations are People too", a double entendre to imply that the actions of people working together create organisations, and that organisations themselves have a personality.

Some people suggest that there is no such thing as society—only people. I disagreed. When people get together to form a club, or a company, or a troupe, a new *person* emerges from their collaboration. I thought it obvious that an organisation like World Vision had a personality different from mine, or from any individual that worked within it.

Second, the international organisation had embarked on a *Core Values Process* under President Tom Houston's leadership—a first-ever attempt to articulate the underlying values of the organisation. What does World Vision believe? What does it stand for?

I had taken part in planning and executing this process. It would bear fruit at a conference in late 1988 where the heads of all World Vision offices met in Warburton, Victoria.

Third, my frustration with organisational inertia. The mass of "The Old Ways" weighed heavily on any attempt to do something new.

"We've been doing it this way for years?"

"It's not broke. Don't fix it."

"We tried that ten years ago, and it didn't work."

I was certain that we needed a circuit breaker. And so, I invented the *Vision Challenge Retreat.*

In the 1980s, the township of Lilydale was the first country town beyond the Melbourne suburbs. The urban sprawl would soon overtake it, but for the time being we could meet at the Bible College Victoria in Lilydale and make-believe we had left the office far behind.

We gathered every staff member who had a management or leadership responsibility. For two days, we tapped into our common feelings and beliefs about who we were and what we valued. It was stimulating and ground-breaking work and I delighted to see so many colleagues involved as leaders and contributors. I felt we may have our circuit breaker. I went home very contented.

About two thousand years before our Vision Challenge experience, Aristotle wrote, "One swallow does not summer make." We may have had a mountain-top experience in hilly Lilydale, but within hours we would be back in South Melbourne.

The key strategy was to roll out the Vision Challenge process in other forms. Our weekly all-staff meeting, Big Devos, was an opportunity to talk about our values in story and example. Since I hosted these gatherings, I looked for every opportunity. Whether announcing a staff change, or delivering a 5-10-15 year service award, or explaining a change in organisational structure or process, I would look for the *values* angle. Much of this was subtle, but somewhere I had learned that leadership is about "consistent action in a single direction." I was looking for every chance to remind us of the values and beliefs we wanted to show through our work.

I proposed a way we could cascade the process throughout the departments, with managers taking the lead to have mini retreats. Mostly these happened in-house for an hour or two. Some departments shut down for an afternoon and got to work differently. When the various State Managers came together for their regular conferences, I joined them to talk vision and values.

The wonders of email were just a few years away, but already we had its precursor. We got an internal email system which, with the right equipment, we could access from outside. One of its delights was the ability to create mailing groups. Something that had been a laborious task for secretarial staff, became automatic. I created a group called "Vision Challengers" comprising the colleagues who were leading the vision change process. I regularly fed them articles about organisational change. Some of the Vision Challengers even read them, which was pleasing.

* * *

28

Be A Drover, Not A Driver

A million leadership articles will define leadership as "consistent behaviour over time". I preferred to describe it as, "keeping the herd generally heading west."

Not too many kilometres from where I live now in South-West Victoria, you will encounter flocks of sheep and herds of cattle on the move. Nearer home, it's long lines of cows meandering in rough single files towards the milking sheds. Further inland a flock of sheep will stop your car while a few Australian Kelpie dogs nudge a hundred sheep from one paddock to another.

If you want to learn leadership, watch a shepherd, or a dairy farmer, or a drover.

Thirty minutes down the Great Ocean Road is a dairy farm owned by friends, Bruce and Jane Pike. One winter, when our grandkids were visiting from the States, we took them to get a hands-on experience of where-milk-comes-from.

Jane met us at the house.

"Bruce has just gone to bring up the cows," she said and pointed us in the milking shed's direction. The teenagers screwed up their noses as the sweet pungency of cow dung welcomed them to life on the land.

"Where's the farmer?" one asked.

"Over there." I pointed at a line of cows half a kilometre off, heading directly towards us.

"I don't see him."

"He's at the back, bringing up the stragglers."

Cows know the way to the milking shed. They make this journey twice a day, every day. Their bodies tell them when they're ready to be milked and they crowd the gate in anticipation of the farmer's arrival. When the gate is opened, they know what to do. They do it. Mostly.

But there are always one or two who are reluctant. Stragglers. Dairy farmer, Bruce Pike, knows each one of his seventy cows. Most he has raised from birth. If there is a cow that seems slow to join the twice-daily march to milking, he understands. He knows why. He knows what to do.

And he leads from behind the herd.

A lot of leadership is like that. Understanding your people. Helping stragglers to stay in touch with the herd.

If a flock of merino sheep interrupts your country drive, you may see another aspect of leadership. The Kelpie dog is rather like the dairy farmer. They can lead from behind, but they will also circle the flock to keep everyone together. And heading in the right direction. Sometimes, a dog will leap over the back of sheep to deal with an uncooperative animal. A few barking reminders, and a paw in the back, do the trick.

Where is the farmer? You will find the shepherd watching from his ute, or perhaps on a quad bike. He'll be on his phone, checking Facebook. Nothing to do here. His work was done when he spent hours and hours training these dogs. He spent his leadership energy and time on staff development. Now he just lets them get on with it.

Back at the World Vision Australia ranch, I learned that most of leadership has nothing to do with grand gestures, but a thousand tiny nudges. Each nudge keeping the herd generally heading west.

The Vision Challenge Retreat was a grand gesture, but what

followed needed to be lots of tiny nudges. One such nudge involved the words we used. Not subtly, I sent a memo off, changing the name of the regular meeting of executives. In my first few weeks in the *first-among-equals* role, I had called it the "Executive Team Meeting". At least it had the word team in it, but otherwise I based the name on the job titles of the people attending.

After the Vision Challenge process got under way, I said I was changing the name to the "Strategy Team Meeting". In a memo I justified the change by saying our "people should be able to contribute irrespective of their place in the organisational structure."

Most of my colleagues understood the message and quickly adopted the alternative meeting name, although they soon abbreviated it to "STM". A couple persisted with the "executive" emphasis (the ETM). Perhaps this showed an ego need, perhaps innate change resistance. In time, common usage overcame old habits. And, more significantly, who attended had more to do with the contribution they could make, than the question of to whom they reported in the organisational structure. Nudging the herd.

* * *

Book 5
Getting The Big Picture

29

When The Mission Statement Is Wrong, Change It

"There's nowhere to park!"

It had not always been so. When World Vision moved into the former "Astor House" in South Melbourne, we had eight storeys of space, plus a two-storey warehouse out the back. After the clutter of the Coventry Street building, we had at last, room to breathe. And after breathing, room to grow.

Although I designed the layout of the Communications Department, I never lived in it. Just before the staff relocated, I moved rather further—to Hong Kong. By the time I came back, World Vision had grown. World Vision staff gradually displaced tenants. How long, I asked, before we needed something bigger?

The symptoms of growth were showing. Burdened by no long-term view of our future, we had allocated parts of the warehouse to staff parking. This was extremely popular. The nearest all-day street parking was far away or full before 7:30am. We had offered one floor of the rear warehouse to Open Family for their charitable community work in South Melbourne. A peppercorn rent of $1 a year was contracted, but never invoiced.

When we needed space to set up fifty telephones to handle the response to television promotions, a few staff car parks disappeared. Soon, I learned the value of "staff benefits".

You could get to the office by public transport. Just a step to the right and a turn to the left off St Kilda Road. An easy ten-minute walk from the place all trains ended up, Flinders Street station. But, since there was parking available, it soon got used up. A few executives had parking spaces, each unsubtly labelled with a job title. For the rest it was first in first served. This standard caused endless complaints.

In a moment of delegatory inspiration, I sent a message asking if anyone was interested in a staff committee to come up with a solution. Thirty-two people raised their hands. I asked these 32 to whittle themselves down to a dozen, and was delighted when they did, without causing a blue. Many saw this act of delegated decision-making as a revolutionary move. I sensed that the word got around that there might be a shift in the management weather.

They proposed, and I endorsed, a roster system that enabled most drivers to get a monthly park at least every second month. It seemed to work for a while, but soon the cracks showed. Staff aggrieved at missing out on this month's ballot would often have to walk past those executive car spaces and see them empty, their owners interstate or out on business. Outrage was gently expressed when a Personal Assistant, familiar with her boss's peregrinations, took it upon herself to put her mini car in his space. (You will notice the gender-specific language of that last sentence. In the 80s, only one of the execs was a woman. Even she had a female PA).

"Car parking is not an entitlement," someone said in an executive team meeting one day. "It's just a benefit."

From the point of view of the organisation, this may have seemed correct. But, after you had battled a greasy, wet winter morning on the trains and trams during the month they'd balloted you off, the sight of an empty parking space, just yearning for your little Datsun 120Y, could cast a shadow over your morning that might make job satisfaction a temporary impossibility.

Where you stand depends on where you sit, and a benefit enjoyed, soon becomes an entitlement.

I yearned for the day when my leadership was not engaged in negotiating car parking issues. I wanted a big convenient building somewhere, with plenty of space because most staff wanted to drive.

Father Bob's visit to my office strengthened my resolve.

"You're tipping us out onto the street. You can't do that."

Father Bob McGuire was the priest of the South Melbourne Catholic parish. And the founder of the Open Family Foundation, whose $1-a-year lease, never claimed, I was ending. Everyone called this modern Saint, "Father Bob", and he was such a selfless bloke that he could get away with being unsaintly when it suited him. A Scot by heritage, he sure was canny.

"Where can we go?" Bob laid on the guilt trip.

"I know. It's hard. But we just need the space."

"You think we don't need the space?"

"No. Of course. No," now I was stuttering. "We're not asking you to move right away. I'm just saying that we will need the space, so you'll have time to work something out."

"Once more, out in the gutters," he moaned theatrically as we shook hands and he left the office.

This felt all wrong to me. Perhaps we had missed an opportunity. What was World Vision about? Why were we here in South Melbourne? What was our mission?

Mission statements were all the rage in the 1980s. Not too long after we moved out of the Melbourne CBD, I recall a meeting where we debated a key objective. We crafted something like this:

> *World Vision Australia exists to raise as much money as possible, at the least cost possible, for projects overseas.*

World Vision was a money-transfer organisation. That is how we saw ourselves. When I was Communications Director, my job was to raise money. As much as possible, within a reasonable cost. We sent the money overseas. We saw ourselves as an overseas aid agency. When someone asked why we didn't support need at home, our usual response was that it wasn't our job. There were many worthy organisations meeting the needs of Australians. Our focus was the Third World.

But the decision to end Open Family's lease burned. It was a decision which I supported and implemented, but we based it on a narrow vision. It made money sense. Open Family's occupancy produced no cash stream. In money terms, there was nothing wrong in the equation. The alternative to termination would mean we would have to rent premises. The cost of keeping Open Family in the house would be the cost of housing World Vision staff elsewhere. That would increase our running costs. The Board read the profit-and-loss statements. Our performance was measured by the numbers.

From my workstation outside Harold's office, with its superior view of the Melbourne Skyline stretching from the Melbourne Cricket Ground (MCG) across the city, I tried to get two things going. I started a conversation about our mission, and I pulled some colleagues together to plan for a future World Vision facility that might meet our needs for more than just a few years.

* * *

30

Where You Stand Depends On Where You Sit

"That was a transcendental conference," he said.

"Transcendental? What do you mean?" I asked.

"Of that conference, no earthly trace remained."

The speaker was Manfred Grellert, a Brazilian who succeeded my colleague, Geoff Renner, as Vice President for World Vision's work in Latin America. Everything from the Texas border southwards.

Perhaps it is best we say nothing about the conference to which Manfred referred—a conference so lacking in on-the-ground outcomes that its deliberations soon disappeared from memory. But it was an invitation from this same Manfred Grellert that provided me real on-the-ground outcomes that would influence my leadership style for the rest of my life.

The setting was Puebla, Mexico, a pleasant drive from Mexico City. The occasion was a regular annual meeting of the leaders of each of the twelve field offices. The agenda contained a half-day for "support office/field office issues" and the President, Tom Houston, would join us. He had a surprise party for his 59th birthday. Someone had booked a mariachi band.

Manfred Grellert spoke at least four languages fluently, or so it seemed to my naïve ears. As a Brazilian, Portuguese was his mother tongue, but he seemed to speak Spanish equally well, and his English was fluently American. His heritage was German, so I presume he knew a *deutsches* word or *zwei*.

Sometime earlier, I had used the phrase "a point of view" during a conversation with Manfred. He had looked at me with a grin and reminded me that a point of view was merely "a view from a point". Manfred's second-language orientation made it easier to see the literal meaning behind the metaphor.

Likewise, when I was learning Cantonese, I discovered that the word for *computer* in Cantonese literally means *electric brain*. I thought that was perfect. Native speakers of Cantonese automatically ignore the literal meaning because they are so used to the intended meaning.

I'm delighted such insights are not copyright. I have repeated Manfred's aphorism uncountable times since.

In a similar vein, Dave Toycen taught me "where you stand depends on where you sit."

One can achieve a lot of understanding by applying these ideas to any debate. The live debate in World Vision during 1986 and '87 was the location of the international office. From the day of its invention, the international office lived with the US office in Monrovia, an Eastern suburb of Los Angeles.

Soon after I joined World Vision in Melbourne, I was intrigued to hear that our international office was in Monrovia. I presumed they meant Monrovia, the capital of Liberia in Africa.

"How enlightened," I commented.

"Enlightened? I don't think so."

"But surely it's commendable for a development agency to locate its international office in Africa?"

"Africa? Are you trying to be funny? Where do you think Monrovia is?"

"It's the capital of Liberia, isn't it?" I was having doubts. "You know, where the Americans tried to set up a new homeland for emancipated slaves."

I learned then, more of the geography of Greater Los Angeles.

In the years before the Puebla Conference, a grand plan had emerged to establish, not merely a separate international office, but an international campus. The site selected was a disused quarry in the further Eastern Angelino suburb of Claremont. The plans were impressive, but the reaction around the World Vision partnership ranged from enthusiasm to gob-smacked derision.

The heat in this argument caused a related discussion to emerge. Whether a global organisation ought to locate its international office *anywhere* in Los Angeles. The common view, at least outside of California, was that L.A. lacked a certain international cachet. We knew it more for Disney, Hollywood and the *Beach Boys*. New York and Geneva were widely recommended as more suitable, with smaller lobbies for London.

"How about Sydney?" I joked.

"It's too far from here."

"Oh. I always thought you were too far from there," I responded, showing my jet-lagged eyes.

It's not overstating the vigour to say, the debate raged. For months.

Finally, the proponents of the quarry surrendered. The international board attempted to quell the location debate with a resolution to stay put in Monrovia.

At the Puebla meeting, President Tom Houston, outlined the board's rationale for its resolution, in summary (and I quote my notes):

- a need for stability in the partnership.
- a need for stability in the international office.
- concerns about reduced effectiveness by dividing the work between Monrovia and Geneva.
- the readily available pool of development expertise in Southern California.
- desire for a Christian image, rather than simply an international one.
- prohibitive moving expenses.
- consistency with lifestyle commitment.

The reaction from our Latin American colleagues in Puebla ranged from flabbergasted to shoulder-shrugging inevitability. Jose Chuquin bravely responded to the fecund air of dismay.

"I think we need to communicate that the US image is a serious barrier to relationships with groups and individuals in our part of the world. Especially on the left of politics."

A wave of grumbling agreement passed over the nodding heads in the room.

Sensing that Jose was stereotyping Monrovia as representative of everything wrong with America, Tom, whose Scottish heritage did not require him to defend the Land of the Free, responded.

"They said of Jesus, 'Can anything good come out of Nazareth?' and, of course, the answer was 'Yes'. Jesus rejected imposing a propagandist or pharisaic stereotype on Nazareth. We should not do that to Monrovia, or the United States. We should be careful not to tell others that nothing good can come out of the US." It was a rebuke, gentle yet clear.

Each of us needed better insight into our own cultural baggage, no-one more than me. The fact is that we see the weight of cultural baggage in others more easily than we see it in ourselves. The more I lived outside of the Australian culture, the more I gained the view of the outsider. And the more I could be appalled by the behaviour of other Australians.

Living in Vienna, as we would do a few years later, we were passing down historic streets of the old central city and overheard an Australian woman announce in loud *Strine*, "I wanna see the church." Somehow, the harsh Aussie vowel sound in "church" demeaned the elegance and magnificence of St Stephen's Cathedral towering towards the sky a few metres away.

Similarly, foreigners often find it amusing that Americans could have a baseball tournament titled the "World Series" when only American teams played in it.

Thinking some theory might soften the debate, I quoted Stanford Professor Raymond Leavitt.

"Professor Leavitt suggests there are two forces that determine an organisation's culture. A *general* force and a *local* force. He says the most powerful *general* force is the society in which it is located. I believe we are making the task of developing and communicating an international image immensely more difficult by locating our international office in a culture which has such problematic implications all around the world."

Someone, perhaps Tom, asked, "What's the *local* force?"

"It's leadership. Tom's role in leadership would be less difficult, if we located the office in a place where the *general* force of the culture was more international in character, such as New York or Geneva."

It troubled me that we were dealing with blind spots. Some of our Latin American colleagues agreed.

"What does the Board mean by 'readily available pool of development expertise in Southern California'?" asked one of the South American leaders. "Have they been to Brazil, India, Kenya? The experts are here, where they are really needed, not in American universities."

Ouch.

"The board says this is 'consistent with lifestyle commitment'. That's just words to me. I don't know what it means. Whose lifestyle are we talking about?"

I did not know whether Tom ever played cricket, but he was cool enough to let these go through to the keeper.

The debate was maturely frank, but I felt sour as we broke for the evening meal. I shared my dismay with Darci Dusilek, Brazil country director.

"I have a feeling we are missing something," I said.

Darci had his mouth full. He chewed slowly. I could almost see him forming an idea with each mastication.

"We are missing the bigger picture," he said. "We do not share a common idea of who we are."

"You mean like a vision statement? I know Tom wants us to work on that."

"That is good." Darci took another mouthful of the chicken enchilada and chewed thoughtfully. I did too.

There was a lot to like at the Puebla Conference. For starters, Latin American people are *fun*. They love to sing and play. There was volleyball, at which I was quickly deemed hopeless and taught to umpire instead. Jose Chuquin, the delightful director of our work in Colombia, loudly blamed "the Australian umpire" whenever a point went against his team.

In the evenings, an informal glee club formed. Various people played guitar or sang. The harmonies were Latino, the guitar work beyond competent. Yet, there was no bravado about their music. This was not performance. It was that old-fashioned round-the-piano shared enjoyment.

"Do you have a song?" asked Tito, holding out the guitar. I was shy to display my rusty guitar work, but there was open encouragement, so I gave them "Waltzing Matilda", and everyone found harmonies in the choruses. When I handed the guitar back to its owner, he said, "Nice chords."

* * *

31

Grab Opportunity Without A Fanfare

I can't remember who said it. I recall it didn't sound like a compliment. "He likes to be the kingmaker."

They were describing the chair of the Australian board, David Jenkin. Frankly, I thought kingmaking an admirable quality. He was on the lookout for promotable people.

David was a decade my senior, with a successful career in retail management with Myer. He moved on to be CEO of the billion-dollar Melbourne Central Development.

We would meet regularly for coffee in Melbourne Central from the vantage of a café overlooking the shopping swarm under the musical clock and dwarfed by the gravitas of the Shot Tower. No-one would have deliberately built a shopping mall around an old tower used for producing lead shot. Confronted by a non-negotiable heritage ruling, Melbourne Central made it a feature. It was a creative solution which spoke loudly of the ability of David and his Melbourne Central backers.

One morning in May, fresh from a few weeks enjoying life with a new son at home, I met with David to discuss the agenda for the forthcoming Board meeting. I always tried to arrive a few minutes early. Skinny flat white was my invariable *tipple de jour*. Without sugar. There had been a time when I loaded coffee with four or more teaspoons of sugar, but the *40 Hour Famine* cured me of the addiction.

"The usual, Mr Jenkin?" That defined cool for me. When the serving staff know what you want, even before you ask. Would I ever be that cool? Twenty years later, long after World Vision days, I would announce my intention to do the morning coffee run to a barista in Yarraville. The habit proved popular with staff of Foodbank Victoria, and the barista always knew my order. OK, not as cool as everyone in Melbourne Central knowing your name and your preferences. One takes ego strokes as they come.

These coffee-fuelled meetings had become routine for David and me since Harold had moved to Sydney. David had a request.

"I think the Board would benefit from a straightforward statement about the directions you and Harold are taking the organisation."

"You mean, like the emphasis on vision and values."

"Yes, but also some clearer statement about how that plays out in management. Organisational structure. Delegation. Training."

"We can do that," I responded, contemplating authoring a short paper for Harold to present. David read my mind.

"You can write it as Executive Team Leader. Harold has talked with the Board about the approach you're taking. I think it would be helpful to have it from you directly."

Yes, please. I liked nothing more than writing memos about organisational architecture. Nerdy, I know. Trouble was, I had learned in these recent few years as *prima inter pares* that words on paper were weak tools compared with actions in the daily battle. What was the point of more words on paper? Look at what I do. Is that not enough?

I have since often wondered, but never discussed with David, whether this was David being kingmaker. David was a member of the Board of World Vision International (and would soon be its chair). Perhaps he knew already that the President, Tom Houston, would not seek another term beyond 1988. Perhaps David was looking a few moves ahead. Perhaps he had a plan for me.

If so, he played it perfectly. There was something to learn here. David could have come clean. He could have told me how he saw the chess pieces falling after Tom's departure.

"Tom leaves. Harold gets the Presidency. There'll be a vacancy in Australia. You should get ready."

He said none of this. And he was right to be silent. He was doing his job of positioning the pieces to maximise the options. He would not hold out false hopes, nor should he. And he may not have talked, only to me.

From this distant viewpoint, one wonders if Ken Tracey, who asked me to write a paper on fundraising in Asia, considered the possibility I might be suited for a job in Hong Kong. Did Hal Barber, the executive Vice-President to whom Ken reported, see possibilities that were yet invisible to a mere player like me?

Of course, they did. This is the job of strategic leadership. Looking down the road. Assessing the possibilities. Preparing the organisation, and particularly your people, to be ready when those possibilities become options.

You need to keep such work close. The merest hint quickly festers into an expectation. Sitting in the noise of commerce, clocks, the clatter of cutlery and cups, David played his role with such perfection I never even got the hint. I heard only a suggestion to write a paper.

This is the paper I wrote.

* * *

MEMO

Date:	7 June 1988
To:	Harold Henderson
From:	Philip J. Hunt
Subject:	Report to the Board from Executive Team Leader

<u>Theory:</u> The most effective organisations are the ones that optimise the use of their peoples' gifts.

<u>Delegation:</u> This means delegating decision-making power, so that our people can use their gifts.

Delegation cannot be abdication. One cannot just say, "You decide." Each manager must have a framework of values and beliefs that guide his or her decision making. This framework is the Corporate Culture.

Delegation cannot be laissez faire. If our people are to *do right*, they must also *think right*. Thus, delegation must have two emphases:

- Helping people to think right; and,
- Helping people to do right.

Develop & Maintain a strong Corporate Culture: If people are to **think** right, we must have, and must communicate a strong, consistent corporate culture.

Everyone in the organisation needs to know, and embody in his/her decision making, the values World Vision holds about our key objective, about excellence, about our Christian holistic approach, about our love for individual people, about our inclusive approach to the Christian faith, about our management style.

The first step is to **develop** the culture. There needs to be a **routine** of forums in which we develop the culture—identified, challenged, refined, agreed.

The **board** needs a planned approach to developing culture in dialogue with the executive director. The preparation for the Council is an existing element in such a plan.

The **executive director** needs scheduled time to reflect on the vision and values of the organisation. Everything depends on the executive director having a clear vision.

The **strategy team** needs a routine of meetings to discuss vision and values. I am sure we would benefit now from a retreat which enabled us to look at issues such as lifestyle, relationships with governments and government intelligence, the fund raising/ community education conflict. We need a planned approach to dealing with these issues.

This is not to diminish the ad hoc development which goes on. We create and teach values on-the-job. We do as we believe. Every encounter of the strategy and operations teams is an informal culture development activity.

We also need activities, probably retreats, which focus specifically on identifying and articulating these values, how they have changed, whether we want them to change, how we shall communicate them.

Once we have the culture, or the desired culture, we need to **maintain** it. You buy the car, but then you need to keep it running.

The most powerful maintenance activity is everyday behaviour. Managers model corporate and personal values in everything they do. That's why some companies think carefully about how their people dress, how they answer the phone, how they build their offices, what executives say to staff in the lifts, and so on.

But there are also many formal and structured ways to maintain the corporate culture.

Internal training is a powerful way of communicating corporate culture. We can choose what to emphasise, and what to de-emphasise. Involvement of senior executives in training carries with it the power of corporate approval. Internal training communicates technical and management skills, but this is not its primary role. The primary role of internal training is the communication of corporate culture.

The Vision Challenge process showed the value for staff of spending time in **retreats**, discovering and clarifying corporate culture.

The content and style of **staff meetings,** department and corporate, communicate corporate culture.

Internal **publications**, such as "Connections", are tools for communicating the values of the organisation. Editors should work with this perspective strongly in view.

How can we be sure that people will do right?

Select the right people. We are good at this. In the first place we choose people to fit the jobs. We don't offer people positions unless we think they have, or can develop, the technical and management skills to be effective.

Also, we encourage people to embark on formal **training**. We have a policy of paying for job-related training for any person who has been on staff for more than a year. We must ensure that people with decision making power have sufficient **resources and information** relating to their work. We have begun this by devolving the budgeting process to department level. Managers now have responsibility for a specific part of the corporate budget and can get real time information on the system about their performance. Our next major challenge is to extend access to information of other kinds. We shall help managers to make marketing decisions based on data that is now locked away in our major sponsor/donor database.

* * *

I don't know what happened to this document. I presume it went to the Board. Its contents were not discussed with me for months.

* * *

32

All Change At The Top

During 1988, the chairs on the upper deck of the good ship World Vision began to move around.

International President, Tom Houston, gave notice that he would not seek another term. His finishing date would be 1st January 1989. The frontrunner seemed to be Australia's own, Harold Henderson and, although he did not hide his interest, Harold expressed doubts.

"The WVI Board is pretty conservative," Harold told me during one of our hours-long conversations. "I think some will not look kindly on my separation." He had recently separated from his wife, Nella. Divorce was probable, and that might not sit well with the beliefs of some Board members.

"Really?" It astounded me that such a thing might be a selection criterion. "Where is the grace?"

"Well, the track record of former WVI Presidents' marriages isn't great," Harold explained. The marriages of the first two Presidents,

Bob Pierce and Stan Mooneyham, had fallen apart during their tenure. Fortunately, the marriage of Tom and Hazle Houston had since steadied the ship. And Ted Engstrom's interim hadn't rocked his relationship with Dorothy.

Despite his doubts, Harold attended a meeting of the chiefs of all the support offices and the senior executive team of the international office. On this occasion, four members of the International Board came along. Although only the Board had the authority to appoint the President, this senior leadership group hoped the Board might take an interest in its opinion. They nominated Harold for a two-year interim term. I understood the vote was unanimous.

It takes a certain amount of *chutzpah* for an executive group to nominate their new boss. There's a chance some Board members might suggest the executives leave the job to them and mind their own business. But, brave or foolish, the matter never came to a vote.

As the meeting of the WVI Board approached, Harold learned that the Canadian Board had instructed their two members not to support him. Also, the four US members were likely to follow suit. Rather than stir up trouble, Harold withdrew his application. It said a lot about the character of this man of peace.

Later the Australian Board Chair, David Jenkin, one of Australia's two members on the international board, told me that the opposition to Harold was not based on his separation or divorce, but on the possibility that he might remarry. Jesus said, "Anyone who divorces his wife and marries another woman commits adultery against her. And if she divorces her husband and marries another man, she commits adultery."

This was 1988. Since then, nothing has changed in the Bible, but it seems more grace abounds these days, because there are many to whom forgiveness rather than judgment is now applied. Including in World Vision, even at senior levels.

The WVI Board still had the sense to appoint an Australian, Graeme Irvine, well-married to Fran. I was sorry for Harold, but glad for Graeme, even though some rocky moments existed in our history.

When World Vision Canada had lent Bernard Barron to start the Australian office, he had not taken long to identify a successor. Ex-YMCA man, Graeme Irvine, was his choice to lead the Australian venture. Graeme's appointment in 1968 proved to be an inspired one. Graeme handed over a well-set World Vision Australia to Harold Henderson in 1975 and took up the international position of VP-Field Ministries during a time of rapid change and growth. World Vision's work expanded in Africa and Asia. Soon we took up opportunities in Latin America and the South Pacific. Growth is rarely delivered without challenges, and World Vision was unexceptional.

The crisis for World Vision began when the Americans lost the war in Vietnam. April 30, 1975 became known as "The Fall of Saigon", although doubtless it had a different name for the victors. World Vision left Vietnam temporarily. Perhaps there were other options, and perhaps World Vision considered them. The withdrawal had ramifications for the many Vietnamese staff left behind. They now bore the stain of association with an organisation linked to the "enemy". Many projects were suddenly without funds. We disconnected thousands of child sponsors from their sponsored children. In aid and development terms, it was a catastrophe.

World Vision's solution was to look elsewhere. It looked to Mexico and the many Evangelical churches through which World Vision might channel support. By the early 1980s, this rapid expansion looked like folly.

My first inkling that there was a problem occurred in August 1982 during my first year in Hong Kong. Around a table in a windowless room at the US office, the International Partnership Planning Meeting resolved to close the entire Mexican operation and reinvent it.

I should have kept silent. Any problems with Mexico had not been on my watch. I did not know what misdemeanours called for such drastic action. I was not a player in the problem, nor in the solution. I was just the kid in the new Asian start-up. But, towards the end of the discussion, I dipped my oar in.

"Look," I said, and everyone looked at me like they had just noticed I was there. "I know little of the history here, but we cannot gloss over the risk to World Vision's reputation. We must *NEVER* let this happen again." I think I did say *NEVER*, in capitals.

Graeme Irvine rounded on me in frustration.

"Where were you?" Graeme shouted. I didn't know he could shout. The words bounced across the table with accusatory force. *Taken aback*, underestimates their impact on me. Graeme glared at me. It felt like a physical assault. The room went silent.

"Where were you after Vietnam, Philip? Where were you when we had thousands of child sponsors calling every day asking about their sponsored child? You weren't here. Where were you?"

The answer was that I was not even in World Vision. It wasn't my problem. I never had to deal with it. Graeme did. And many of those around the table had sweated blood to make the best from a critical situation. And later, when it proved not good enough, they sweated again to fix it. They didn't need some newly minted corporal critiquing their work.

Fortunately, time heals. Graeme and I never became besties, but we worked together effectively in the following decade, particularly during his time as WVI President. I enjoyed the evident reality of his Christian faith. Graeme had a rich stream of spiritual depth that enhanced his leadership, both in character and effectiveness. I often think he was perhaps our best President, and I wished our relationship had been better from the beginning.

Graeme became President in 1989, although those upper deck chairs on the World Vision juggernaut began shifting a year earlier.

During Tom Houston's hand on the tiller, he had persuaded Graeme to take up a new position in Geneva. The task was to reposition World Vision with the World Council of Churches, Lutheran World Federation and UN agencies headquartered there, such as UNHCR, the refugee agency. The common view of the politically minded was that this might sideline Graeme, but few argued that he was not well-suited to the role.

With the President's position settled on Graeme, Harold was keen for something different. He agreed to occupy the Geneva seat. This made sense given Harold's background in church life and polity in Sydney, and his now two decades' experience in World Vision.

One seat remained vacant. *CEO, World Vision Australia.*

* * *

33

An Empty Chair Is An Invitation

Since my return to Australia, much had changed. The *MCG* had become the *'G*. Unleaded petrol and power steering were common. A few hectares of bushland at the bottom of our hill had become Bayswater North, decorated with the architectural fashions of the late 80s and a maze of curving streets.

A full fifteen years after the birth of Melanie, our third child, Richard, came into the world. Suddenly all our lives changed for the better. Judy loves her babies, even when they have some of their own. As a Dad, I loved nothing more than rocking Richard off to sleep at night or sitting him on my thigh in my home office while I wrote emails with my spare hand. At fifteen, Melanie stepped up to the role of deputy Mum which trained her well to produce four terrific grandchildren later. And at sixteen, Jamie became an instant Big Brother, unless a nappy needed changing.

Away from home, our executive group had experienced some

changes. Dave Toycen, who had succeeded me as Communications Director, left to be second-in-command in World Vision Canada.

I was not alone in my disappointment when Dave left. He was creative, driven and compassionate and we had always been close. Carrying an American label in Australia is not always an advantage, but Dave was a farm-boy from the American Mid-west, and he blossomed in Australia in a job that gave his talents free rein. With Warwick Olson from our Ad Agency, Dave made friends with people who mattered in the Australian media. Their relationship with Bruce Gyngell, the first face on Australian TV and by now head of a British television network, was just one of many door-opening achievements.

"I'm sorry to see you leave, mate. What made you decide on Canada?" Dave answered indirectly. It surprised me.

"*You* did, mate," he said. "I thought maybe I'd have a shot at the CEO role here if Harold ever moved on. Then when you came along, I guessed the Board would prefer an Aussie."

Nothing wrong with Dave's logic, but perhaps more portentous than even he imagined. Not only did Dave prove to have more freedom to exercise his talents in Toronto, but he was the obvious choice when the position of President of World Vision Canada became available. He served there with distinction until retirement, three decades on.

I promoted Dave's deputy, John Rose, to replace him. Probably the easiest people decision I ever had to make. John was the obvious choice to everyone. He had worked alongside Dave in a Deputy Director role after spells within, and later managing, our representative team. John was a born organiser and a thoughtful manager who would serve in this role until the end of my tenure. World Vision later invited him to become the international VP Communications. We are life-long friends.

Rowland Croucher and Geoff Renner were two other additions.

A decade and a half earlier, Geoff had worked with Graeme Irvine in the YMCA. He pioneered World Vision's work in New Zealand and then became Regional Vice President for Latin America. He had an impressive CV and a library of corporate knowledge—in his head. Harold invited him to join our team to give strength to our work at the sharp end. Also to oversee government relations and to develop a Public Information and Community Education function. True to form, Harold created the role around Geoff's gifts.

An Empty Chair Is An Invitation

Coincidentally, Rowland Croucher had been my Pastor for one year that we worshipped at Blackburn Baptist Church. As Judy and I had become increasingly bemused by the unproductive debates post-union in the Uniting Church, our friend, Robert Colman, invited us to Blackburn Baptist "just for a night". That one night became the entire year before we left for Hong Kong.

Rowland had left Australia at about the same time for a Senior Minister role in Canada. It had been a mistake. Harold had invited him to join World Vision Australia having no specific job in mind. As Harold did.

Harold had a knack for talent-spotting and, if I learned anything from him, it was that outstanding leaders design jobs to fit the talent, not the other way around. Too often we write a job description and try to squeeze someone into it. I learned and practised, the alternative. Appoint the person who best fits, then reshape the job description to make the most of their gifts. For Rowland, a vague charter of Church Relations soon blossomed into a major program of leadership enhancement in Australian churches. Full marks to Harold's intuition.

The Hunt family lived in Boronia, a working-class suburb in the foothills of the Dandenong Ranges, East of Melbourne. Our foothill rose 10 metres closer to Heaven than the surrounding terrain and most of the residents referred to it, with satirising pretentiousness, as "Boronia Heights". Our steep streets hugged the hillside curves, and much of the original bush had been kept. We could see the TV towers of Mount Dandenong from our house and a few minutes' drive up narrow roads would take us into fertile forests and hippy hamlets of the Dandenong Ranges. The town of Belgrave, far removed in style from its British namesake, sat at the end of the train line and the start of country living. We had a memorable meeting there.

Kevin Gray, our Finance and Admin Manager, lived in Belgrave and offered his lounge room for one of our regular "Strategy Team" discussions. Harold chaired these meetings and he made himself the first order of business.

"Last week, the Global Leadership Team made a recommendation to the international Board that they appoint me as President for an interim 2-year period." Harold confirmed what we already knew from the efficient office grapevine.

There were sincere affirmations from the team and some questions. Harold expressed his doubts.

"Whatever happens," Harold concluded. "I have decided it is time for me to move on. I've communicated this to David."

"Has David said how the Board is going to go about choosing a successor?" asked Kevin.

"Not yet."

Then Rowland spoke. "What process is the Board going to go through to get the input of the executive group on the leadership question?"

"Don't know. They may wish to look outside," Harold observed.

"Do we think they should?" Rowland addressed the group. "If we think the best candidate is in this room, I think the Board should know that."

I felt uncomfortable. Nervous. I knew that years in leadership in the Baptist Church had taught Rowland political skills. Churches will do that to you. And this felt like a manoeuvre to expose what otherwise might stay invisible. Even without my saying it, everyone in the room knew I would put my hand up for the job. Who else would? Rowland himself would be a fit candidate. Geoff would offer. Perhaps there was merit in getting all this out in the open. The relationships in the group were not so fragile that we couldn't handle the discussion. Yet, I felt we were being manipulated. I believed the numbers in the room were mine. That meant it wasn't fair to Geoff. But then, maybe I was wrong about the numbers.

"Do you think you could reach a consensus?" asked Harold.

"We should try," Rowland replied.

"It will be hard," I said, "but it'd probably be good for the team to attempt this." I wasn't sure if I based my motivation on my best interests or the team's. We looked at each other. Everyone nodded.

It required plain speaking. I said, "Well, I would like to think I'm the best choice." Geoff showed his interest. Rowland said he had other goals in life and wouldn't put himself forward. So, Geoff and me. The team began a healthy discussion about our respective histories, some comments about differences in management style and emphasis. The consensus was for me.

The result affirmed me, but I got more delight from the maturity of the team in the manner of our discussion. It is hard to pass objective judgment on one's peers, but we spoke truthfully, and I detected no intent to derogate any person. Harold reported the next day to Board Chair, David Jenkin. Amazed and impressed, he said that no secular management team could have accomplished such a task without destroying itself.

Nevertheless, I felt uncomfortable about Geoff's feelings. The next day I made the snap decision to talk it out. After dinner at home, I jumped into the car and drove across the darkening suburbs to Doncaster. Geoff was just finishing chairing a seminar. Down the road at Nunawading Denny's, we drank average coffee and talked.

"What will you do if I'm appointed?" Geoff asked.

"I'd be looking around," I admitted. "I'm sure I could work with you, but I'd feel like I was going backwards. I'd want to move forward. I'd prefer to stay on in some useful role until I had something to go to, but I'd understand if there wasn't a place for me."

"Fair enough."

"But what about you, Geoff? I'd be wanting you to stay on in your present role. You're driving our thinking on improving our relationships with the field. I don't want to lose momentum. We could work together with the Hong Kong and Singapore boards, too."

Geoff didn't seem to need any time to consider the matter. "I'd like to stay on."

We wished each other best of luck without saying, "May the best man win." We said nothing more on the matter for the next nine weeks.

Decision Day came. The Australia Board meet quarterly for a day. Harold's position had only become clear two days before. Not our President, but the international Board had appointed him to the Geneva post, VP International Relations. He would resign as Australian CEO at the Board meeting. David Jenkin had completed his own schedule of discussions including two lengthy meetings with me and, I presume, similarly with Geoff. On the afternoon agenda: whether to appoint me or Geoff, or whether to hold open the decision and look outside.

Over 150 staff wanted the news. I'd be lying to say I wasn't stressed.

"Can I tell everyone that you will announce the Board's decision today, whatever it is?" I asked David. "I can schedule a staff meeting for 4pm and you tell us where the process stands. There's been so much speculation and it's not good to let the matter drift. Even if the Board have an external search, it would be best to tell the staff immediately. Otherwise it will affect morale." David agreed. I emailed: *Staff Meeting @ 4pm*.

I attended all Board meetings in my Executive Team Leader role since I was the person most across Operations and had the ready answers. About 2 o'clock I got the nod from the Chair to depart. I saw Geoff, telling him they were "onto it."

"Do they want to talk to us?" Geoff asked.

"They haven't said."

"I asked David to allow me to make a presentation," he explained. "I said they should interview both of us, with our wives."

Wives? I thought. *They've already met Judy many times. Anyway, she's not the candidate.* I thought it an odd idea. Already old-fashioned in the 80s.

"Well, David will call us if he wants presentations. I better make some notes," I joked, although, as Geoff well knew, we were both prepared.

Board members told me later that David gave a comprehensive report on his discussions with the executive team, including me and Geoff. The Board then talked about whether to open up a search process or select from Geoff and me. A vote decided, not unanimously, to select from the internal candidates. There was more discussion about this, and finally they appointed me, unanimously.

Outside, corridors were being paced. The clock said 10 minutes to 4. I was composing a note for the Board. "If you want to cancel the 4 o'clock staff meeting, better say now, or it'll be too late". David emerged from the Board meeting with a face that gave nothing away.

"The staff meeting can go ahead," he said. "You should come into the Board meeting." A good sign. I hoped.

The Board invited me to accept the position. I did. David left the room to let Geoff know. There was a brief dialogue between me and the Board members of which I can only remember the closing comment from one member, John Denton.

"Well, looks like we are in for interesting times," John said. I wanted "interesting" further defined, but suddenly David returned, and we were off downstairs to the Staff meeting.

We arrived downstairs at 4:15 and someone had led singing of Scripture songs. Then John Bergin, an ex-staffer opportunistically present, was giving everyone an update on the progress of his many-times-almost-dead daughter now recovered from a series of heart problems. Quite a story. Worth having the meeting for that alone.

Harold told everyone that he had accepted the international position. Then David made a longish speech, finally announcing that the Board had appointed me. Warm applause spread into a standing ovation. Very moving indeed. Then I made a fair speech, also too long, and called Judy with the news.

"Congratulations," she said, "They've done the right thing."

Our life didn't change because I had become CEO of Australia's largest aid agency: it changed because we had a third child. Richard was six months old when he attended my Commissioning Service in the World Vision meeting room in December 1988. I was forty years old.

Just as Jamie and Melanie had changed us in surprising and joyful ways, Richard brought that unique refreshment that comes with a baby in the house. It also introduced us, over the next decade, to a whole fresh bunch of friends—the parents of Richard's friends. Since many of these Mums and Dads were having their first children, while we were having our last, they were a generation younger. Young friends keep you young, just as late children do. Without a late child, how else would I discover *Silverchair* or *Linkin Park*? I had become accustomed to my car radio being switched to Double-J or Triple-R. Now it was Triple-J, while Triple-R endured.

My job title changed nominally on appointment. Nothing much else changed. I continued to live comfortably in a workstation outside Harold's office. And when my job title changed officially on 1 January 1989, I went on vacation for three weeks. If this was symbolic of a work-life balance decision, so be it.

* * *

Book 6

Got The Gig, Now What?

34

Clean The Curtains, Share Out The Real Work

I have two sisters. One on either side. At the time of my elevation to the glories of Australian leadership, they, along with my parents, lived in Sydney. The younger sister lived under the flight path of Sydney airport. Mum and Dad lived just near the Drummoyne Cricket Ground. The older sister lived in Blaxland in the Blue Mountains, which is quite a walk from Circular Quay.

Judy has two brothers. One on either side. The older one was living in France, the younger in Brisbane. Her Mum and Dad lived on the Queensland Sunshine Coast with a view of the northern tip of Bribie Island.

With our recently expanded family, we had planned well in advance to spend the New Year in Sydney and points further North. So, on New Year's Day, ostensibly my first day as CEO, we loaded up our Holden and enjoyed a few weeks of meet-the-new-cousins. Along with meeting our baby Richard in the flesh, we were also to meet Suzanne, latest (and likewise last) offspring of the younger sister (under the flight path) and Anna, latest (and second-last) offspring of the younger brother.

After trying to not think about work for three weeks, it was with great anticipation I rolled into the same old parking spot under the same old South Melbourne building, rode up the same old lift to the same old eighth floor and settled into the same old swivel chair in front of my same old workstation.

Judy Moore, my able personal assistant, and later a super field worker in some of the world's toughest places, asked, "Well boss, what do we do first?"

"First, we don't call me boss," I replied with a grin.

"Come on," Judy urged, "there must be something new we can do."

I leant back. Lots to do. But nothing new. A pile of documents appeared in my in-tray from my three-week absence. Internal emails cluttered my in-box. Nothing new or remarkable.

I swivelled around and looked at Port Phillip Bay through the window. The IBM building was still there, a block away. That funny round tower with the Mercedes-Benz logo had not changed.

I pulled focus and looked at the scrim curtain that hung between me and the glass. Gosh it was dusty. Was someone responsible for getting the curtains cleaned? I had no idea.

"Let's get these curtains washed," I said.

"Yes, Philip," Judy replied.

"Much better."

While my revolutionary decision to do some housekeeping went little noticed, there was momentum in World Vision Australia in January 1989. Since my return from Hong Kong, there had been income challenges. This was a first in our history. Until the 1984-85 year, donations had grown every year. Never a single setback. Until the post-*Band Aid* hangover.

Someone called this "Compassion Fatigue", but that was wrong. A surge of a single group of supporters was the cause. I called them "The Occasionals", although the marketing folk called them "one-time donors". There are many people who may be sympathetic to a cause and will give only when they see something on mass media. These days, we may supplement mass media with various social media, but Mark Zuckerberg's parents had only recently invented him.

Clean The Curtains, Share Out The Real Work

Occasionals give occasionally. In the 80s, that meant whenever there was good mass media coverage. We didn't care who was talking about world poverty; we always tried to join the conversation. As the Australian audience got to know us better, as we moved towards becoming a household word, a portion of the response to mass media inevitably flowed our way, whether or not we advertised.

In the *Band Aid* year, we enjoyed an immense surge in *Occasional* givers. The following year, the occasion to give had already passed for them. We budgeted badly. Our income fell short of plan.

Entering the freshly curtained world of 1989, we were again enjoying surfing the income growth wave. The first three months of our year were right on budget, and well ahead of any previous year. Our spirits were up. It was a good time to be in a new chair, even if it was the same one.

In the last few months of 1988, apart from the changes at the top, felt by many in the organisation apart from me and Geoff, we were hosting the International Directors' Conference.

From all over the world they came. The leadership of World Vision offices from the entire planet. About 200 people from 57 countries descended on Melbourne for a fortnight. They spent the first week visiting supporters around Australia, and the second week at a conference centre in Warburton, a 40-minute drive past the wine fields of the Yarra Valley.

We had no experience in organising events of this size, but staff stepped up. A committee formed under the leadership of HR director, Merilyn Hill. She recruited twenty of our best organisers who, by the way, still had their proper jobs to do. Everything came together. Staff met our visitors at airports and billeted them in their own homes. The Hunt family welcomed the Field Director from Peru, Carlos Garcia, who seemed to enjoy the week with us in Boronia, despite our mutual disabilities in each other's mother tongue. Carlos enjoyed being Uncle to baby Richard and gave him a Peruvian beanie as a memento.

A dozen years later, I noticed that Carlos had become Second Vice President of Peru. As a leader in the Baptist Church, Carlos was influential in gaining the votes of Evangelical Christians. This undoubtedly helped President Alberto Fujimori to win his first election.

However, two years in and Fujimori was looking every bit the dictator. In April 1992, Fujimori, supported by the military, disbanded the government, fired judges, and suspended the constitution. This must have been too much for Carlos. He took refuge in the Argentinian embassy. Fujimoro ruled for another eight years before impeachment caught up with him. Convicted on charges of murder, bribery and embezzlement, they sentenced him to 25 years in prison.

Wikipedia tells me that in 2002 Carlos Garcia was "decorated by the Congress of the Republic of Peru with the Medal of Honor in the rank of Grand Officer, 'for his commitment to the truth and his permanent struggle in defence of democracy.'" In 2017, Fujimori was controversially pardoned and released.

All the men and women who attended the Warburton Conference had credentials like Carlos. Without exception, they carried their fame and history lightly. Heroes at home, they came as modest travellers to Australia, a place foreign to them.

Warburton was a master class. So much experience. So much knowledge. So little hubris. I was a twelve-year veteran of World Vision but felt like a newbie. My role was to keep a record and produce a report. With more bravado than confidence, I designed a discussion to clarify and agree on the Core Values. When it worked exactly as planned, no-one was more relieved than I.

The Core Values Process represented a break from normal World Vision practice. Too often we had mistaken *representation* for *participation*. They are not the same. Through the leadership of the incoming international President, Graeme Irvine, we debated the Core Values in many forums, at many levels, in many places. There was a year-long converging-diverging process. Converging to representative events like the Directors' Conference, or the Partnership Executive. Then diverging to more parochial forums like regional directors' meetings, local boards, local staff executives, often right down to front-line staff groups.

It had worked well. A few wise heads noted that we were an organisation that preached participatory development. So, why had it taken so long to practise it?

No sooner had we watched the last of our visitors disappear down an aerobridge than I was flying to London for a meeting of the international marketing and communications colleagues, chaired by

Harold Henderson, in his newly minted role of Vice-President for International Relations.

At the end of the conference, Bruce Gyngell generously lent us his personal chauffeur (and BMW735i) for a drive in the English countryside. In Cambridge, we stopped for lunch and a wander around the colleges. The chauffer delivered us to the door of the eatery and asked when he should return.

"Right away, mate," we insisted. "You're invited. Australians don't leave the chauffeur in the car."

I polished off another idea before my job title officially changed. I called it "Trellis."

In the days before social media, information in an organisation often depended on the rumour mill—the grapevine. Some leaders see the grapevine as a problem. I saw it as an opportunity.

Just before attacking the long haul up the Hume Highway north, I spent an hour designing a newsletter. I called it "Trellis" and sketched a masthead—a bunch of grapes espaliered on a wooden trellis. Underneath the masthead were the words "Supporting the grapevine." For the next eight years that I led World Vision Australia, staff would find a single double-sided newsletter on their desks once or twice a month. *Trellis*. Two pages. Two columns a page. Stories. News. Results. Celebrations.

Blogging—1980s-style.

* * *

35
Listen To The Stories You Tell

Give a man a fish, you feed him for a day.
Teach a man to fish, you feed him for a lifetime.

Educate a girl, educate a nation.

You can't do everything, but you can do something.

Slogans, proverbs, aphorisms and cute stories saturate the development aid world. One of my favourites is the Starfish story:

> *While walking along the beach, I see an old man by the edge of the surf. He bends down slowly, protecting the muscles of his back, and picks up a starfish that has washed ashore on the high tide. As I watch, the old man stands*

> *erect and frisbees the starfish in a long arc into the calm water beyond the shore break. He walks on. A metre or two. Stops. Reaches down and picks up another starfish and repeats. The starfish falls satisfyingly in the surf beyond waves that might bring it back to shore… and doom.*
>
> *The old man is drawing himself up for another throw as I get near enough to ask.*
>
> *"Why are you doing that? There are hundreds of starfish on the beach. And tomorrow there'll be hundreds more. On thousands of beaches."*
>
> *He looks at me. My comments do not surprise him. "True," he says.*
>
> *"Throwing them back can't make a difference," I insist.*
>
> *The old man looks down at the starfish in his hand. Slowly, he leans back and launches it into the air. It lands safely, just like the ones before. He turns to me.*
>
> *"Made a difference to that one."*

Sponsor a child. Make a difference to that one. It's a noble sentiment, but is it enough?

There is another story, "The Parable of the River". There are many versions on the Internet, just as there are of the Starfish story.

> *There is a village by a river. One day, a woman washing the family's clothes sees a baby floating by. She calls for help, and soon others come from the village to rescue the baby.*
>
> *A few days later, another baby floats by. And then the next day, two more. And within a week, villagers are rescuing two or three babies daily from the river.*
>
> *The village organises a watch on the river. People modify their houses to care for the babies. Women volunteer as wet nurses; villagers supply food. The local priest blesses the caring work of the villagers and says prayers regularly for safe rescues. Village life goes on.*
>
> *One day, someone asks, "Why don't we put a team together and go upstream to see what is causing these babies to be floating in the river?"*

World Vision began in the 1950s, rescuing babies from the rivers of war in Korea. Few people regarded our work as anything less than necessary, worthy, perhaps even noble. Children were being orphaned by the war. Right-thinking people, many of them Christian, established children's homes to care for these abandoned waifs.

World Vision didn't invent sponsor-a-child. Other organisations, notably Foster Parents Plan (now known as PLAN) had been doing it for years. But there was no patent on fundraising concepts, and soon World Vision was sponsoring many children in South Korean orphanages.

While I was still spinning disks on Brisbane Radio, World Vision had already realised that caring for the welfare of children in institutions had downsides. Feeding starving kids sounds like an excellent thing. And it is. But there were *upstream* issues. Why are these kids starving? If we don't find out, soon enough they will starve again. How to break this cycle?

A seminal training conference gathered some of World Vision's key project practitioners in the early 1970s. Held in the emergent post-colonial reality of the Philippines, World Vision people were introduced to new ways to think about aid and development, and new ways to tackle poverty. At its source.

Emergency relief has its place. If my child were starving, I would want her fed. Right now. Don't waste time telling me you're working on stopping the war. She needs food. *NOW*. World Vision never abandoned emergency relief. It expanded its portfolio. Working alongside communities in identifying the causes of poverty emerged. Community development workers trained in being *alongsiders*. Using tools to identify causes. Responses that were home grown and appropriate. Growing a community's ability to provide a sustainable future for their children. A future that didn't need World Vision anymore.

In my lounge room today, hangs a Chinese scroll. On it, in beautiful hand-written Chinese characters, is a poem. Twenty lines in four-character sets. Nothing I have read about development more succinctly captures the essence of community development. Here is an English translation:

Go into the crowd
  Live with them.
Study together.
  Share in their ups and downs.
Be in the same boat and help them build up themselves
  according to their understanding.
Guide them in truth,
so that they will practise what they have learned and not
  just become an empty vessel.
In doing so, you will become their true friend.
Do not upset laws and orders,
  But discern what is the priority of life
  Then you will never regret.
Be kind to all and gently lead the young
  Until they accomplish their tasks and enjoy their
  fruition.
So the people will all say,
  "We have achieved the goal ourselves!"

I don't know which Chinese philosopher wrote it. Nor how ancient it is. I know that it summarised what I was learning about leadership as I accepted the invitation to lead World Vision Australia. Practitioners of community development see their method in it. People, like me, involved in organisational change and development, see ourselves in it. Leaders who want to leave a legacy could take the poet's advice.

Fast forward fifteen years from that conference in the Philippines. World Vision had discovered that moving from a single model of development to a broader, more sustainable form, hadn't been easy. We complicated development sometimes, by a narrow definition of community and, particularly, the place of the local church within that community.

For a Christian organisation, it appears unquestionable that we like to work with Christians. Almost invariably, this meant looking for a local Christian church and working with them. Often, field offices were under pressure to expand their programs faster than might be prudent. Success in fundraising produced dollars. Extra dollars meant more projects. Growing too fast has consequences. Consequences that took time to show up.

Often, projects with churches seemed to have no end in sight. They were welfare-oriented with no real community ownership or engagement. World Vision had funded some for over thirty years. The partnering church considered this a permanent arrangement.

I had visited some of these projects from our base in Hong Kong. We called them "Rice Christian" projects. If there was any benefit (the rice) to be distributed, the people came to church. In some places, failure to attend weekly Bible Study got you struck off the beneficiary list. Some pastors were more motivated by the opportunity to fill their church pews, and too many wanted the project benefits to only flow to Christians in their church. In some projects, "honorariums" funded a range of standard church activities like worship services, Vacation Bible Schools and "representational" expenses, which seemed to apply to anything the pastor spent. More than one pastor appointed himself (yes, nearly always men) as Christian Education Director and took a salary.

There was a distinct pattern about the way these projects started. A pastor becomes the founder of a church by moving into the community. That's OK so far. Many people with a heart for the poor insert themselves into a community. To "go into the crowd, live with them." It's how many missionaries work. It was the next step where things might drift off the straight and narrow.

World Vision signs the pastor up for a project and not-too-subtle coercion gets the local people to join their church. After a few years, if challenged, the pastor says, "But if World Vision doesn't fund my project, I will lose my church. Without the project, the people won't attend." A goodly number of us in World Vision considered this a spurious defence, but some others took a more benign view of these projects. One sometimes heard the comment, "Well at least these people are hearing the Good News. They wouldn't hear about Jesus otherwise." The end justifies the means.

I distanced myself from this sentiment. If the only reason people came to church was to receive the project benefits, then had they really "heard the Good News of Jesus"?

Most communities had more than one version of the Christian

church in their community. Churches without World Vision projects found their flock drifting away. They called it "sheep-stealing". Project funds were a source of power and influence in communities. And not being used for the right outcomes. Many of these pastors had no interest in developing community leadership for the simple reason that it could undermine their own.

The decade of the 1980s was a period in which we turned around many of these unsustainable projects. Fortunately, there *are* pastors who care more about the development of their people, than in building a little empire. Tin emperors were gradually defunded. In many other places, representative community groups gained control. We started projects from scratch with better methodologies.

We were still rescuing those babies in the river, but we now worked on the causes of infant flotation. Communities empowered. Children benefited. Families prospered. A better kind of community-based development emerged as World Vision's central work. And the Good News of Jesus was preached in actions. And when necessary, in words.

* * *

36

Find A Vision That Empowers Everyone

I'm occasionally referred to as "the guy who invented the *40 Hour Famine*". It's a myth. Not even close to the truth. I think World Vision Canada invented it, but they may have borrowed it.

I joined World Vision in 1976 soon after the first state-wide *40 Hour Famines*. The Communications Director was David Longe, a marvellous, energetic man. He was one of these guys who had a thousand ideas before breakfast. He would arrive in the office about ten o'clock (he hated early starts), by which time I was working myself up to cope.

But like so many creative types, David was not a born organiser. I worked with him over two years translating his ideas into actions.

One of his ideas was a national *40 Hour Famine*. Later, we accepted this event so readily as part of the calendar, it was hard for most of us to imagine what a scary idea this was in 1976. But David had a vision. A vision of hundreds of thousands of Australians slamming the fridge door. A vision of thousands of groups meeting in schools and church halls to bed down for an overnight fast. A vision of the media leading their nightly bulletins with the news that most of Australia was starving for the day. A vision of our political and entertainment leaders falling over themselves to identify with the World Vision *40 Hour Famine*.

David Longe's vision of the *40 Hour Famine* remains his most enduring legacy. It started with an idea. An idea clearly articulated.

It was such a clear vision, that all I had to do was write it down and assign responsibilities to various people to put it into action.

"If people think right," said Dr Ted Engstrom, "they do right." Dr Ted was still President of World Vision US when I moved into the CEO office Down Under. His managerial style had served World Vision during the time it was outgrowing its disorganised beginnings. He had taught a thousand or more managers how to manage right. His rubric was Management by Objectives, a structured, sometimes rigid method of planning and execution.

I still remember where I was when Ted told me, "If people think right, they do right". We had been to a World Vision function during one of his visits Down Under and I was driving him back to his hotel. As we waited to join the freeway, we talked about World Vision rethinking our vision.

"If people think right, they do right. It's really that simple." Even while implementing MBO in his organisation, Dr Ted had liberated hundreds of workers by this rule of thumb.

"If people know what the organisation is supposed to do," he said, "and if they share the right values, they will do the right thing."

"You make it sound easy, Dr Ted." He was never just plain Ted to our generation.

He chuckled. "You think?" We shared a grin. "It's the toughest job in the world. Getting people to think right is hard work. Too hard for most leaders. So, they try to rule by policies, and systems, and regulations. They kill innovation. Not to mention job satisfaction."

Certain words were weaving into our conversations about organisational purpose. As if transported through the air-conditioning. Empowerment. Transformation. World.

Before Tom Houston handed over the international Presidency

Find A Vision That Empowers Everyone

to Graeme Irvine, he had shared an idea about World Vision being a bridge.

"I borrowed the image from our New Zealanders," he admitted. "World Vision as a bridge between supporters and the poor." I pinned my childish sketch of this bridge to the fabric of my workstation wall. Another advantage of modular office furniture.

"What do you think of that?" I would point at my bridge drawing.

"Is it one-way traffic on the bridge?"

"If it's two-way traffic, is it just money one way and thank-you letters the other?"

"Where's Jesus? Directing traffic?"

"I don't like 'supporters' and 'the poor'. They don't seem balanced ideas."

And on and on. And round and round. But with a purpose. To find a statement of purpose. World Vision Australia already had a purpose statement when I became CEO. We called it our "key objective".

> *The key objective of World Vision Australia is to raise as many resources, with a minimum of overhead, to make ministry possible.*

The statement had the advantages of being short, neatly balanced in three parts, measurable and easy to remember. But there was a problem. It reduced our work to dollars and cents. It was purpose-built for accounting.

Gradually "World Vision as bridge" grew into a sentence. I printed a WordPerfect Presentations slide and pinned it to the wall. It read:

> *Empowering People to Transform their Worlds*

By now, our many discussions imbued these words with meaning. We could answer the question, "What does this statement mean?" It became part of our orientation, and the tagline appeared in our publications. I hoped that the fullness of its meaning would deepen as we used it.

Our talk became part of a larger conversation at the 1989 WVI Council. The meeting resolved that the language of our traditional statements was less adequate for our changed understanding of our work. Some folk liked our statement. A few didn't understand it. Lots of folk liked some bits of it and not other bits. Some missed the point that transformation was not something only in community development projects in distant lands, but also ought to happen among supporters here at home.

"People in Australia need their worlds transformed, just as much as people in Uganda," tripped off my lips more than once. "Maybe more," was often the response. Indeed.

I made only one change to this purpose statement during my time as CEO. We added a single phrase at the beginning: "Fighting Poverty by". It became:

Fighting Poverty by Empowering People to Transform their Worlds

Charles Clayton, CEO of our British counterpart, suggested, "It clarifies that we are in the poverty fighting business. Without these three words, it could just refer to a school, or a church, or a computer company." Good input. Gratefully accepted and integrated.

When new staff met for orientation, I unpacked this purpose statement, to reveal the layers of ideas it contained. I would begin by dispelling the idea that we were in the fundraising business.

"The problem is that too many people see World Vision in Australia as just in the fundraising business. And they probably see World Vision India in the fund spending business. Both views are inadequate. Too narrow. No, wherever World Vision exists, it needs to be in *one* business. And that business is fighting poverty by empowering people to transform their worlds."

Then I would enumerate each of the components of our mission statement. Nine Poverties. Two People. One Transformation. Four Worlds. Many Empowerments

"What sort of *Poverty* are we fighting? Well, the Bible describes various types of poverty." And I would list the nine different Greek words that describe poverty or things that cause poverty. Things like oppression, meagre wages, people worn down by toil, those who work for their daily bread.

Two people? Well, that was easy.

"The *Supporter* and the *People* in Project Communities. Both are our customers. We must not serve one at the expense of the other."

Find A Vision That Empowers Everyone

What *one* transformation do we seek? Nothing short of Jesus' vision of the *Kingdom*. A vision of the new heaven and the new earth. An abundant life of true peace. Of right relationships: Person to person, Person to God, Person to the environment.

Four *worlds* need transforming.

The world of the *Heart*. Transformed emotions. A feeling of compassion for the poor. A concern for the impact of the consumer society on the rich.

The world of the *Head*. Transformed minds. Better understanding. Knowledge of issues of world need. Understanding of the interconnections between the rich and the poor.

The world of *Horizontal relationships*. Transformed inter-personal relationships: love for the neighbour. Redistribution of wealth; that's one reason we raise funds. Social justice: communities accessing ways to work together. Transformed relationship with the created order; yes, WV is interested in the environment.

The world of *Vertical relationships*. A right relationship with God. World Vision is interested in evangelism. Not as a component of projects, or a department in World Vision, but as a dimension of transformation that the Good News brings to every individual touched by our Christian ministry.

And finally, *many empowerments*.

Information can be empowering. Sponsoring a child in another country can empower a change in understanding. Inspiration can empower you to move. Opportunity provides the way.

It was important to get our frame of reference right. We now understood we were doing fund raising **because** it fought poverty by empowering people to transform their worlds.

We were doing development education **because** it fought poverty by empowering people to transform their worlds.

It involved us in political advocacy on behalf of the poor, **because** it fought poverty by empowering people to transform their worlds.

We wanted to reveal the Good News of Jesus, **because** it fought poverty by empowering people to transform their worlds.

* * *

37

Inch By Inch Anything's A Cinch

Apart from cleaning the curtains, there was much to do in that first year. I wasn't in a hurry. My intuition was that too much change too soon would be counterproductive. I needed to get comfortable with my extra responsibilities, even though I felt ready, well-prepared. More important, the surrounding people needed to adjust to me, even if they already knew me well.

Leftover commitments peppered my diary from the year before, when my responsibilities had been fewer if not altogether different. I needed to find a new balance. I felt I had the luxury of a stable team doing impressive work. More listening, more talk. Fewer surprises. This was my agenda.

Returning from the January holidays, and after cleaning the curtains, the senior management team met off-site for two days. Without too much talk about changes at the top, we reshaped the edges of the new relationships subtly, almost without noticing.

International visitors continued to find their way Down Under at two or three each month. This never changed. When possible, I would take them for a drive into the Dandenongs, have lunch and discuss our agenda while looking at the scenery. Manfred Grellert, VP for Latin America, later joked, "Be careful when Philip takes you for a drive. He entertains you with lunch, then hits you with the hard questions on the drive home."

Usually, at least one group within the organisation would come together each month. Volunteers, State Managers, and the various departments. Usually, I would attend for part of the time, even if I had no obvious agenda.

April found me in Quito with the Field Directors of Central and South America, followed by a week in Nairobi, and a day in Harare. I arrived back to celebrate Judy's birthday and a day doing radio interviews and the Ray Martin TV Show. The next day took me to Sydney.

Chairing the Board in Hong Kong continued, as did the Advisory Group in Singapore. Lausanne 2 took me and a bunch of colleagues to Manila for a long week in July. The Global Leadership Team met for a second meeting, and the WVI Council met in August.

The Council met in its reformed shape in 1989. Three years earlier it had adopted the recommendations of the Bylaws committee that I had served as its secretary and report writer. Our work had been on the right track. The balance between *fundraisers* and *fundspenders*, between support and field, had dramatically tilted. The field voice was loud and valued.

I was attending my third Council meeting. In 1983 I had attended as the recently fledged CEO of World Vision Hong Kong. I was short a few feathers and rather awed by the variety and quality of the attendees.

The WVI Council of 1986 brought the Bylaws process to a rewarding conclusion, together with a successful moment of stand-up humour.

At the 1989 Council, Australians popped up at every turn. Some of us were a little self-conscious about this and tried to keep a low profile. Perhaps this had a fortunate consequence. When Australians contributed, they made contributions of the highest quality. It was a highlight of the Council, and not only for the Aussies.

David Jenkin was the Council Moderator. He drew the most praise, and rightly so. He set the scene from the first bounce. His opening address was a clear call into the future. He called World Vision into discovering and doing Christian holistic ministry. He urged us to empower people to transform their worlds. This was music, familiar to my ears.

He spoke of a world-changing ministry in which supporters and the people in project communities would be changed. He called us to take environmental issues seriously. God gave us stewardship of the earth and God expects responsibility. He asked us to be a bridge between the rich and the poor. More than that, we should be bridge crossers. A glance at the audience provided my first tear-choking moment as I saw so many heads nodding in agreement. We heard David's statement of praise and hope repeated throughout the Council, "What a strategic ministry we have!"

This Council was much more participative than previous lectern-centred experiences. The afternoons of the first two days offered nine elective workshops. They randomly allocated us to the electives, which raised eyebrows, including mine. My favourites were disregarded, but I came to see the wisdom of the organisers. Unfamiliar territory stretched us. It also meant that *expert* cliques did not dominate any discussion. They split the experts up.

There was one jarring note. Most people obeyed the allocation rules even if they failed to get their first choice. This was not true of the men allocated to "Women in Development and Leadership". They opted out into other workshops. It appalled me. More was to come. Reporting back on the first day, John Allwood from South Africa, being the only male in the room, had been invited by the elective to act as recorder. *Well done, ladies,* I thought. John light-heartedly rebuked the recalcitrant absentees. This seemed to trivialise the issue. Sometimes humour works against you.

His censure had no impact on attendance on the second day. I thought this might cause the group to feel marginalised. They produced a report with an extensive list of recommendations. The first was that women's membership of Boards be increased from the present 12% to 40% by 1992. The Council laughed. Yes, there was actual laughter.

> *Strategy for radicalising a movement:*
> *1. Marginalise them. Isolate them. Let them work on their own.*
> *2. When they say something, ignore it. Better still, ridicule it.*

This radicalisation strategy works every time. The result is the same whether one is talking about the African National Congress or the Women in Development and Leadership Workshop.

Few things got me worked up at Council. This got me angry. Had we not learned anything about the Women's Movement in the last 20 years? Women like Joan Levett (from the Australian Board), Roberta Hestenes and Colleen Townsend Evans from the US Board tried to calm me down. They suggested the laughter was not derisory, but the result of anxiety. Not directed at the women or their suggestions, but in response to a realisation of how much we need to understand and do. I thought them much too generous.

The radicalisation of the workshop could have resulted in a demands posture. Such a posture would cause a legalistic approach. We set standards, quotas. Sometimes this causes mistakes, like hiring someone because they meet the affirmative action standards and discovering they cannot do the job. We needed to walk the hard path between ignoring the issues and doing nothing, and a too-legalistic approach. Part of the solution? Find the right *woman* for the job. I rejected the rationalisation that we look for the right *person* for the job. We needed a clear affirmative intent to increase the number of women in senior leadership. In Australia we needed to look at the Board and the Executive Team. Theory aside, we knew that one never finds the ideal candidate, but one often finds candidates that bring different strengths and weaknesses to a job. Affirmative action then means selecting the most qualified of these who is also a woman.

The Council had a half hour plenary discussion of the resolution presented two days earlier by Joan. This was necessary but frustrating. I had the good luck to be absent for part of it. Perhaps this was God's way of keeping me quiet. Or the Devil's? The Council adopted the resolution in full. But they added four words to one recommendation (look for the underline):

> *Recommendation 4 LEADERSHIP: The implementation of succession planning programs, to identify, select, and train females <u>as well as males</u> with aptitude and potential to fill senior management positions as they become available.*

Really? This carried. The Moderator said it was "Unanimous", but I fancied he overlooked the abstainers.

I liked to think I was a feminist, but I wasn't. I learned to be male as a boy in the 1950s and '60s.

Australia was then, even more than now, steeped in patriarchy. Everyone in leadership was male. Granville Central Primary School teachers—all male. Parramatta High School teachers—mostly male, although Miss Brown, my English teacher, could out-teach, out-inspire and out-control them all. Wavell State High School—a better balance (we're in the Sixties now). Brisbane Boys' College—definitely all blokes.

The leaders in the Methodist and Uniting Churches we attended, were men. I worked under men in the National Bank, at the three radio stations that employed me, and at World Vision. Not until the 21st Century did I report to a woman, and even then, the reporting relationship was to a Board chaired by a woman.

But in the 1970s there was a tiny gleam of feminist light at the University of Queensland. I was majoring in Journalism (under male lecturers and tutors), and Language of the Media, an amalgam of English studies focussing on language and style. Required reading for this latter mélange was *The Female Eunuch*, by Germaine Greer.

The problem with social conditioning is not so much that it is powerful, but that it is invisible. I was lucky to dabble with a minor in Sociology which introduced me to ethnomethodology—the study of taken-for-granted norms and behaviours. For example, there was, in the 70s, a taken-for-granted rule that adults did not sit on the ground. At a railway station, if all the seats were occupied, everyone else stood. Mums even ordered small children to "get up off the dirt". By the turn of the century this ethnomethodology had gone. Every millennial sat on the ground.

Similarly, there are taken-for-granted rules that become standards through common use, which is why, in the United States, all the light switches work upside-down—to an Australian, anyway.

I found Germaine Greer heavy going. Over in the journalism tutorial we noted how a teen-girl magazine named *Dolly* (yes, really) was chewing on the borders of stereotypes. I bought each issue and submitted a content analysis study as an assignment.

The following year, I enrolled in a sociology unit titled *Sex Roles in Society* which took a tutorial/discussion format led by a mid-30s woman in a series of long flowing dresses and attended by fifteen students. One of those students wasn't female. Me.

In December 1989, I gathered our managers together for a retreat. I called it the "Core Values Retreat." A year earlier, the Warburton Conference had settled on the five big ideas that should shape our organisational values. These were:

> *We are Christian*
> *We are Partners*
> *We are Committed to the Poor*
> *We are Stewards*
> *We are Responsive*

Having the list wasn't much use unless we could see these values lived out. What does it mean to be *stewards*, for example? I wanted everyone at World Vision to have an answer. And I knew that wouldn't happen if I only made speeches about it.

Instead, I selected five people to take one core value each and invited them to design an interactive learning event. The goal was to explore what each core value meant, and how we would see it lived out in World Vision Australia. The famous five were not our most senior people. I didn't want a top-down approach. All of them, in my estimation, were much better suited for the task than I, and so it proved.

Over two days, I felt a new vibrancy emerge among us. There were no wallflowers. The shy were talking; the loquacious were listening. Executives sat on the floor; junior managers held the whiteboard markers.

Towards the end of the retreat, I urged everyone to take this experience into their own teams. Explore the core values with everyone. I felt certain they would set about it with enthusiasm.

Did they? Yes, some did, and some did not. The process had been the right one, but I realise now that I missed a step. Following up. Somebody needed to be monitoring the trickle-down process, ensuring that there was carry-through. That was a task I could have easily asked from one of our HR colleagues.

Inch By Inch Anything's A Cinch

And so concluded my first year as CEO of World Vision Australia. Among the pleasant news to take forward into the last decade of the 20th Century was the financial report. World Vision Australia's first quarter income had exceeded $10 million for the first time.

* * *

38

Only Collaborate Where You Don't Compete

"We need a good disaster every year." Speaking was one of the finance people at an international meeting. There was an intake of politically correct breath around the conference table.

"You want to rephrase that?"

We knew what he meant. From an accounting standpoint, an earthquake in Latin America, or a tsunami in Indonesia, meant a sudden rush of income. An aid agency isn't like a for-profit business. More income doesn't mean more profit, because most agencies plan to spend everything they raise. If we kept money aside at the end of the year, we spent it later. Recovery from a disaster might take five years, but we might raise most of the income to pay for the recovery within a few weeks.

World Vision was Australia's best known and largest aid agency by 1990. Whenever the media reported an emergency, thousands of Australians turned to us to deliver their gifts. Naturally, every other agency was advertising. You could not open a newspaper without finding advertising from World Vision, Save the Children, Community Aid Abroad, Freedom from Hunger, and dozens more. Even tiny agencies most people had never heard of, would take 3 columns by 20 centimetres to tell their story and ask for money. This gave rise to an experience that played out over the next few years. An attempt at inter-agency collaboration.

It was ironic that people saw aid agencies as competitors. On the field, there was lots of collaboration. Earthquakes, floods and wars happen, and they leave legions of suffering people looking for more help than their governments can deliver.

One organisation, usually a UN agency, would take the coordinating role in a disaster scene. Regular meetings involving all the actors resolved potential conflicts. They allocated work according to agency ability and strengths. One agency might concentrate on food delivery while another might try to deal with water and sanitation. Another might concentrate on providing shelter. It wasn't always happy families among the agencies, but there were friendly, professional relationships. And a few romances.

But, at home where funds were being generated, it looked like a battle for attention. A competition for money. "It's not a good look," we were told. And, "there are too many agencies," which was something hardly ever heard about soft drink brands, or cigarettes. As a marketing person, I had applied the rules of effective advertising to World Vision as if it were any other product. If it worked for selling chocolate, it should work for selling World Vision. And it did.

But appearances matter, and so we soon found ourselves in inter-agency meetings. And World Vision was not everyone's best friend. This was a consequence of our size, but also of our behaviour. We had focussed on our own task. We were successful. We had given little attention to the community of aid agencies. Other agencies did not see us as joiners.

Collaborating as a community came to a head in late 1989 with the showing of a John Pilger documentary, *Year Zero: The Silent Death of Cambodia*. I was quite a fan of Pilger, enjoying a small share of his iconoclastic political views, so I was enthusiastic when I saw that the documentary was about to screen. We had had some moderate success with television advertising, and John Rose, our Communications Director, wondered whether we might place an advertisement at the end of the program. Our agency went ahead booked a spot. Reflective of my own rather self-referential standards, it never occurred to consider whether Pilger already had relationships with other agencies.

A day or so before the program broadcast, I was the target for an outraged phone call from John Pilger. He advised me in vitriolic language of his commitment to Freedom from Hunger and suggested we should hand over the funds. If I said anything in response, I doubt it. It may have been reasonable on some scale of ethics to pass over the income, but John had asked for the wrong remedy. He should have asked for the names.

Names matter to fundraisers. The first rule of fundraising is that someone who has given you a donation is most likely to do so again. Much of effective fundraising is based on maintaining the relationship with the donor. I'd agree fundraisers don't always do that as well as we might. One-off donors are good, but long-term and regular donors are diamonds.

ACFOA, the peak body for aid agencies, had only recently invited World Vision to its Executive Board. Foreign Minister, Gareth Evans, suggested ACFOA needed to be more representative of the aid sector. Despite the efforts of colleague Roger Walker to represent us in the national forums, we never were elected to the board. World Vision was simply not popular. Perhaps our size and rapid growth made us a threat. I wanted this to change. Chief Executives of other agencies were on the ACFOA Executive. Roger could represent us well, but I felt the symbolism of the CEO would send the right message. My strategy was to keep quiet, listen much and cooperate as much as possible.

The Pilger/Cambodia appeal tested our resolve and was not without ripples. It wasn't long before a request came to share the names and the funds. We were reluctant, but I urged the colleagues to suffer for the sake of better inter-agency relations. We suggested various alternatives. They rejected all. Reluctant, we accepted proposals put to us regarding sharing the income and the names.

Simpler for some agencies than others. In our case, name-sharing meant writing new software. No-one in IT had seen this request coming. Other agencies interpreted our delays as deliberate reluctance. One *ingénue* vented his spleen by writing to all agencies plus Pilger himself, accusing us of reneging on our agreement and implying malice aforethought. This disappointed more than shocked me, for this was how many regarded World Vision. It needed to change.

We quickly hosed the bright spark into a pouting ember, and a more productive discussion emerged around whether we ought to try again. Over many meetings we agreed the major agencies would form IDEC, copied from a British model. My memory is that IDEC was an abbreviation of International Disasters and Emergencies Council; it was only ever referred to as IDEC. This organisation would make public appeals on behalf of the named agencies which now numbered twelve. Seemed like a way forward.

Soon enough a disaster helpfully came along. IDEC advertised prominently in newspapers and received free coverage for the day or two that television news covered the story. IDEC members were free to appeal to existing donors.

Then the difficulties began. There had been some agreement about evenly dividing up the income. That enormously advantaged the smaller agencies. This pleased them. For World Vision, it seemed we were being penalised for being cooperative. Some within World Vision thought this was a price worth paying. I admit to not being one of them.

I believed that World Vision would have run a more successful campaign in our own right. Agencies appeal in different ways, and the combined message erased these differences. The advertising was too safe and unemotional. Disasters were disastrous, after all. But this was a side issue. I wanted the names.

And that's where it all fractured.

Since all the responses were through one campaign, albeit with a list of known agencies, it was impossible to tell which agency brand might have influenced the response. It was even possible that people thought IDEC was a new agency altogether. Some might have responded out of genuine dislike for other better-known organisations.

The people who had responded were not just present supporters, but future ones. But only if properly followed up. We debated. We could match names against our own databases and follow up any matches. Perhaps we could divide the balance equally. Someone suggested we turn IDEC into an agency and run it as a joint enterprise. I sighed and shook my head in dismay. I'm sure my face looked like one of those eye-rolling open-mouthed sideshow alley clowns.

Only Collaborate Where You Don't Compete

The experience revealed a fatal flaw. One cannot imagine Pepsi and Coke cooperating to sell a single cola drink and share the profits. The drink could be neither Pepsi nor Coke. It would be a new product. It would compete against Pepsi and Coke. The companies would compete against themselves. How would Pepsi and Coke agree to share the profits? How would they assess the relative contributions of the two companies to the new product's success?

IDEC's irony was that there were better ways for development aid agencies to work together. Lobbying the government for more development money. Collaborating on public interest campaigns. Jointly producing educational materials. Doing and publishing research into the effectiveness of aid. Developing Standards of Performance and Outcomes for the Aid and Development Sector. And much more. These things we were not doing well enough.

Competitors should collaborate where they don't compete. Not *vice versa*.

My recollection is that we agreed to send out a common thank-you letter and invite each donor to say whether they would like to receive further information from one or more of the cooperating agencies. I can't remember whether that happened. I do remember that the next time IDEC activated, World Vision demurred and let the others go their own sweet way. Soon IDEC became just another chapter in a book.

* * *

39

Make Money Decisions That Work

Own or Rent? 343 Little Collins Street was the World Vision address when I joined in 1976. I loved working in the middle of Melbourne. Lunchtime had me exploring the lanes and arcades or wandering through the Myer emporium. We occupied two floors at the top of a building on the corner of Little Collins Street and Elizabeth Street. We rented the space.

Most businesses pay rent rather than owning their building. For them it makes sense, because rent is a cost of doing business. Costs reduce profits. Reduced profits reduce tax.

But World Vision is a not-for-profit organisation. It exists for charitable purposes. It does not pay income tax. It soon became clear that rent was a bad proposition. It would be better stewardship to own a building, than renting one. In 1978, World Vision bought 29 Coventry Street with money borrowed from a bank. Within four years, when the building was too small, we sold it for a profit. That profit, supplemented by a new loan, bought the building at 161 Sturt Street.

Now, in the late 80s, it was time to move again. We would move for the third time in twelve years. I didn't want this disruptive pattern to be permanent.

I had no experience in real estate, apart from buying the family home. I had been on the periphery of any previous decisions about facilities. I needed a committee with some proper experience.

Fortunately, we had on our Board, someone who knew one or two things about buildings. When Myer Emporium built its first big shopping mall in the 1960s, it looked to a staff member, Vic Upson. The result was Northland Mall in Preston. Two decades, and more shopping malls later, Vic was a member of our Board. He was delighted to help, and I formed a committee around him. Geoff Renner was a shoo-in owing to his history of securing a site in Auckland for the New Zealand office some years earlier. Max Warren was our Facilities Manager so he got a guernsey, and they needed Kevin Gray for the numbers.

"Let's find a building we can live in for ten or fifteen years," I challenged the committee.

Access for staff was an issue. Our South Melbourne location provided good access by public transport. You could walk to the office from Flinders Street Station, although the trams were regular and quicker. While most of our staff came by train and tram, many said they would drive if only there was somewhere to park.

We mapped where our staff lived. The answer was everywhere. A few lived in the soon-to-expand area around Werribee, but most lived in the Eastern suburbs. We tried to find the centre of our staff demographic. The pin descended on Camberwell. Vic's committee discovered that the population centre of Melbourne was somewhere near Monash University. And moving towards Cranbourne at two metres a year.

Over the next couple of years, we looked at several buildings, East of Melbourne. Some staff liked the fact that other agencies occupied offices in "more suitable" suburbs. Community Aid Abroad, later Oxfam Australia, were in Collingwood. Perhaps we should look in Footscray? I liked the image of being in a less commercial environment, but the price for this satisfaction always proved enormous.

After many existing premises were offered, inspected and rejected, we finally found something that might work. Radio Australia was moving from their purpose-built facility in Burwood East to a new ABC home just down the road from our Sturt Street office. Radio Australia's Burwood East building was a long two-storey boomerang, angled across a green field facing the morning sun rising over the Dandenong Ranges. It was almost exactly the right size, and I loved the thought of living in a mostly horizontal building, rather than a tall, thin one. There would be plenty of parking for staff and visitors, room to expand the building, and not much internal renovation to make it all work for World Vision. We did sums. We couldn't make them work.

Radio Australia lived on part of a huge undeveloped block of land that had once been MacRobertson's chocolate factory. Later, the Tally-Ho Children's Home was there. When we moved to Melbourne, we used to take the church youth there in the winter for swimming in their heated indoor pool.

This was to be the future site of World Vision Australia, but we didn't know it yet. We discovered the answer, by thinking about another problem.

Our family was attending Doncaster Church of Christ and it was facing growth problems. There is a rule-of-thumb in church accommodation that the limit to church growth is 80% of your seating capacity. We were already beyond 80% and signs of discomfort were visible.

Renovate or relocate—this was the strategic question.

As part of that process, a few of us speculated whether a joint development project with World Vision might work. The Doncaster site was near the huge Shoppingtown development. It was valuable. Perhaps a high-rise building that incorporated offices for World Vision, other tenants providing an income stream, together with a church and car parking?

Some back-of-the-envelope calculations over coffee with my Board chair, David Jenkin, didn't advance the idea. It sparked a different idea instead. We had already determined our answer to the renovate/relocate challenge. For World Vision, relocate was the only viable solution. Yet we had not found the ideal place. Space and time were both running short.

Meanwhile, every day I drove along Burwood Highway, past a huge green paddock where the highway intersected with Springvale Road. On the corner across from the Radio Australia building, a developer had begun work on a business estate. One office block caught my eye as just about World Vision sized.

I turned my Holden down the serpentine access road, assessing the building's dimensions. Yes, it looked about right. A For Sale sign wore an "Under Offer" stripe. I walked outside the deserted building, finally arriving at the front door.

"This is perfect," I mused. "God's gift for World Vision." I put my palm against the glass door and said, not too loudly, "Hello God. I claim this building in Your Name." Smiling at my private joke with the Almighty, I continued my commute.

Within a week, the tenants arrived and had their name proudly displayed in metre-high lettering. PHILIPS.

There's a verse in the Bible that says, "The effective prayer of a righteous man can accomplish much." But if this was God's response, it was way more than I expected. Surely, just an amusing coincidence.

Nevertheless, there was a further irony within a few weeks that showed that maybe God was keeping World Vision in mind.

David Jenkin, in the rest of his spare time, was chair of the board of his local church, Blackburn Baptist. Our family had attended there before the flight to Hong Kong. This church was also suffering growing pains. And the rest of the old Tally-Ho land was for sale. It was a huge allotment. Big enough for more than half a dozen multi-storey office blocks. Even if we joined World Vision's needs with Blackburn Baptist's we couldn't make the sums work.

We needed a third-party. A housing developer stepped into the conversation, and within weeks we made a successful offer for the land.

We subdivided the land between the three parties. I named the access road "Vision Drive". Blackburn Baptist built their new church, Crossway Baptist Church. The National Archives of Australia bought a lot from us at the end of Vision Drive. We began work on 1 Vision Drive—a building that would serve our purposes for decades, rather than just a few years. One more move, and our moving days would be over. Not only that, but we would have room for car parks, and a second lot in case we ever needed a second building. My immediate plan for this well-grassed paddock was to offer it for agistment. I loved seeing horses so close to the office.

We only made one mistake with the building. In hindsight, I should have insisted we build on the horse paddock, placing the building away from Springvale Road. We built a concrete slab building that was two-storeys tall on Vision Drive, but viewed from Springvale Road travelling South, the full three-storey edifice commanded attention. It stood there alone in a large paddock. It looked big. And expensive. It made a statement that didn't sit right with me.

As other office blocks were built along Springvale Road, its prominence became less of an issue, but for a while, its very presence begged a question. How could a charity afford such a thing? Some passers-by would answer wrongly, but the right answer was arithmetic. It was the cheapest solution. Cheaper than renting from day one. And, when we paid all the debts, World Vision owned a rent-free building it has now occupied for almost thirty years.

* * *

40

Trickle Down Theory Of Imparting The Vision

I spent much of my life as CEO of World Vision, finding ways to "keep the herd generally heading west". There is no one thing you can do to achieve leadership goals. There is no one-time vaccine you can administer. What's required is a complete package, a hundred small actions, consistently applied. That's what it takes.

Our new home at 1 Vision Drive had a lunchroom. Actually, one whole side of the building's ground floor was an enormous room that we reconfigured with movable walls. We dedicated one end of it as a lunchroom for staff with tables, lounges and a marvellous view across a lake.

Here on most days you could find a game of 500 going on over sandwiches. Four players would gather, and latecomers would slide in, hoping for a hand. I would often join them. I had no particular strategy in attaching myself to the card game. I just enjoyed playing cards. But I soon realised that people noticed that when their CEO was in the building, and when his agenda was not wall-to-wall meetings, he ate lunch in the lunchroom—like everyone else.

Trellis, the blog that appeared on everyone's desk at frequent intervals also became another way of communicating the vision and values. And there were lots more ways.

New staff benefited from orientation. An hour of hearing about who we were, and why we were here, and what we believed, and how we behaved. Or tried to.

Every few months, the latest bunch of recent arrivals would find an invitation to come to my office for morning tea. I had a workstation in one corner, and a round table in the middle of the room. Around the table, with tea or coffee, and some cake or biscuits, I would ask the new folk, "Why did you want to work here?"

Actually, I wasn't quite that blunt. I would briefly tell my own story of how I came to join World Vision. A desire to apply some knowledge and skill in a for-purpose organisation. But I also suggested there were lots of reasons one might join up. Just needed a job? Liked the idea of working for a charity? A friend worked here? Even, perhaps, a vision from God in the night?

Around the table we'd hear our stories. It was easy and, after a few minutes, comfortable for everyone.

Big Devos had become the standard name for our weekly staff meeting. It was a combination of worship songs, prayer, announcements and a speaker or perhaps a video. If I was in town, I always hosted and read the announcements. I tried for humour and only once or twice did my jokes get out of line. Every comedian needs a "too soon" moment. We always welcomed new staff warmly and farewelled old ones kindly. Often the announcements highlighted news that I might develop further in *Trellis*.

Each department started the day with their own devotional time, but often this was honoured in the breach. It was not something I wished to impose on managers, and some were better at making it worthwhile than others.

From time to time, we would invite a random bunch of colleagues to join me for lunch at Fasta Pasta down Burwood Highway. We chose each group so it comprised people whose paths didn't normally cross during the working day. There was no fixed agenda except that I would often ask someone "What's your story?" to get the conversation rolling.

Trickle Down Theory Of Imparting The Vision

I learned something to my advantage from every one of these pasta-fuelled meals. And many staff appreciated the time together.

The management team was mostly composed of those who reported directly to me and met regularly for our own training and planning. Often, we would move off-site for more intensive work.

An opportunity to bring the Australian Board together with the New Zealand Board, resulted in two live-in retreats during my tenure. Board members otherwise only met 6 times a year, for one day. The agendas were all-business. How was a Board member to get an insight into the genuine work when we filled their agenda with memos and spreadsheets?

Some of our Board members visited World Vision's work when they travelled. There is no substitute for seeing World Vision at work in the field. These Board retreats proved to be significant culture shaping and learning experiences for all who attended.

I liked to walk around the building whenever I could. I soon discovered that this was an actual management technique with its own abbreviation—MBWA: Management By Wandering About. Sometimes it was just being seen that served a useful purpose. The CEO not closeted in their corner office. Often, a random conversation gave me an insight or helped to sort out someone's concern.

Mostly the main culture-shaping activity was just to be boringly consistent. I often felt like I had said the same thing a hundred times, but the truth was I had said the same thing to a hundred different people.

Be boring. It's an essential technique.

* * *

41

Integrity Is The Bedrock Of Reputation

Year of the Horse, 1991, had galloped into life. Richard would become a talkative two-year-old, entertaining us by renaming television personalities. So, Jennifer Keyte became Jeffiner de-Keyte, while Steve Vizard became Steve Visors. Melanie entered Year 12 and Jamie graduated into the hard world of job-hunting, soon securing work at Agmedia, the compact media unit of the Victorian Department of Agriculture. Although Agmedia disappeared in budget cuts a few years later, the experience of video production set Jamie up well for a career on the production side of television. In the meantime, he discovered snowboarding and developed an expertise in making friends around the world.

But before the working world consumed my days, we had our last-ever family holiday. All of us crammed into one minivan to tour Tasmania. We flew into Launceston, toured the North Coast, and drove across the Apple Isle in a single day to Hobart, finally spending a day at Port Arthur before flying home. Port Arthur, soon to become notorious for a mass shooting that changed gun ownership in Australia, was better known by me at least, as the temporary residence of William Hunt, sentenced along with his brother and my direct forefather, Richard Hunt, for English crimes. No trace of William remains in Port Arthur.

In the rarefied air of the upper floors of Sturt Street, South Melbourne, ideas were bearing fruit. We had long seen the benefit of staff visiting actual projects in field countries.

I knew the value firsthand. My first exposure to how World Vision worked had been in the aftermath of a tidal wave in East India. My job, with no experience to my name, was to guide a Willesee-At-Seven film crew, anchored by reporter, Howard Gipps. It had been foundational to my respect and admiration not only for World Vision workers, but for the amazing fortitude and generous kindness of the very victims of the disastrous tsunami.

"If only we could include a field visit with every employee's orientation program," I may have mused more than once. Colleagues were working on the idea quietly. Soon a policy emerged that allowed staff to accrue one leave day a year for field ministry orientation. World Vision would cover on-ground costs of such a visit and allow half of the airfare be covered by payroll deduction.

In March 1990, Channel 4 in the UK broadcast a documentary titled *In the Name of Hunger*. It was not kind to World Vision, nor to the development aid sector.

The television program focussed, not on World Vision in the UK, but on World Vision Germany, accusing that organisation of misreporting finances, inappropriate benefits to senior staff, and unreasonably high administration costs. Immediately, the international office pulled together a task force of Canadian and US-based accountants and sent them to Germany to investigate.

The program echoed tabloid television in *A Current Affair* style. All the techniques of the propagandist were on show. Harold Henderson, now Vice President for International Relations and based in Geneva, was interviewed with a low camera angle, suggestive of a hidden camera, yet he had freely given the interview. Rather too freely, perhaps.

Integrity Is The Bedrock Of Reputation

Soon after watching this attempted demolition job, Peter Philp, our in-house media man, appeared in my office.

"Mark Colvin. *Four Corners*," Peter said with ominous enthusiasm.

"What's he want?" I asked. As if I didn't know.

Peter's one-word answer wasn't the best thing I'd heard that day.

"Hancock."

Mark's work was already well-known to me. He was a clever and intelligent interviewer, and I felt my body temperature rise when he let me know he had just watched a copy of the *Dispatches* program. It was a measure of Mark's journalistic professionalism that he began this way, giving me warning about what his line of questioning might be.

I did not yet have the advantage of the World Vision investigation, and my answers to Mark were probably unhelpful. I knew my lack of facts would sound evasive. We wondered what the *Four Corners* team would do with the material. It would not be the first time they had scheduled a *Dispatches Exposé*.

A few weeks later a copy of the investigation arrived on my desk. I was pleased to read that they found no evidence of personal gain by management or board members. Their auditors now reported that as far as they knew, no other charitable organisation in Germany declared actual expenses as openly as World Vision Germany.

We were tempted to send the report off to Mark Colvin, but there had been no follow-up interview and I decided it may be better not to stir the pot. I was reasonably confident that should *Four Corners* take the matter further they would be on my door for an interview.

Criticism hurts when it is blatantly false or biased, but, in my heart, I knew Hancock's venom was merely misdirected. World Vision did have an integrity problem, and it did have to do with money.

In 1990, World Vision still operated on accounting assumptions based on that original Korean girl that our first President, Bob Pierce, had agreed to support. The story about World Vision's beginning was told by Bob in a 1983 book. During the Korean War, Bob took a movie camera and combined preaching with moviemaking.

> "On an offshore little island, the Dutch Reformed Church had a school for girls and a hospital. ... The missionary, Tena Hoelkeboer, had heard the simple way I taught the university students, and she wanted me to do the same for

> *the children. In the simplest language I knew I told them who Jesus is and how God loves them. ... Then I gave an invitation to any of them who wanted to know this Jesus. ... I told these kids, 'Go home and tell your folks you're going to be a Christian.'*
>
> *"Well, when I came to the mission school the next morning, Tena met me with a little girl in her arms. The child's back was bleeding from the caning her father had given her when she went home and announced she was a Christian. ... (Tena) threw that little girl right into my arms and lashed out at me."*[1]

To his credit, Bob was stunned by his own cross-cultural naivete and admitted it. Tena had children in the mission school she was already sharing her food with. She couldn't take one more. Bob looked in his pocket and produced all he had—five dollars. Tena took it and told Bob to send her five dollars every month and it would be "fine."

And so, as far as Bob thought, he (or perhaps Tena) had invented Child Sponsorship. Bob soon invented World Vision, a typically grandiose name for a tiny American organisation based in Portland, Oregon, but such was the post-war American enthusiasm for setting the world aright. For five dollars a month World Vision would send your $5 to a child in a Korean orphanage.

Come forward forty years and World Vision was raising funds in a dozen currencies. Institution-based child sponsorship projects were a tiny minority, replaced by a complexity of short-term emergency relief, long-term development, government funded projects and more. And within each of these categories we could describe sub-categories almost to infinity.

We nailed the international budget down each year in the awkwardly named "International Affairs Committee". The major support offices were members. The fundraising side totalled their numbers for the forthcoming year and sent them to the international office. Likewise, did the project delivery side. The accountants crunched the numbers, and we had a plan.

But something rather important seemed to get lost. The relationship

---

1   Franklin Graham with Jeanette Lockerbie, *Bob Pierce: This One Thing I Do*, Word Books, Waco Texas, 1983, pp. 72—73.

Integrity Is The Bedrock Of Reputation

between the individual donor and the project they were funding had become less clear. From the point of view of the completed world-wide budget, everything looked balanced. The forest of numbers looked fine, but there was a problem at the level of the trees. Some dollars that supporters gave for Purpose A were actually being used to subsidise Purpose B.

Some of this cross-subsidy looked ethically OK. For example, careful language communicated that funds raised in the *40 Hour Famine* were used in a variety of ways. But World Vision could hardly use funds provided by the Australian or US governments to subsidise something else. These funds came with their own fine print.

This lack of clear correlation between donor and project had been part of my motivation for support and field offices to work together in project and marketing design. The Dispatches program may have helped the more relaxed in World Vision to look again at our reputation risk environment.

I'm told the view over Lake Lemond from the conference centre in Glion, Switzerland, is breathtaking. For the three days that brought together the international cadre of World Vision marketers, the lake was invisible through impenetrable clouds. These conferences always attracted my still beating marketing heart even though my colleague John Rose, and our agency man, Warwick Olson, were more than capable of representing us. But I had joint responsibility with Chris Radley, the agency man for the UK office, for one agenda item.

Chris and I were to present our findings from the two explorations to Brazil and Kenya (see chapter 16 "Child Sponsorship needed Fixing"). There we had seen projects that featured genuine community empowerment. The early signs of genuine change showed benefits for sponsored children, and the entire community. The US and Canadian offices had abandoned child sponsorship as a marketing method and now regretted it. Inevitably they returned to the tried and proven link-with-one-child method of child sponsorship, and I had high hopes that they would show interest in work that Chris and I had done some years prior. Like grass after a bushfire, the ideas were just waiting for rain. With the aid of Chris's witty cartoon PowerPoint, we offered ideas for helping sponsors to experience the reality of project life and the evidence of sustainable development.

We were brilliant, of course. And, of course, everyone nodded, shrugged shoulders and went to see if the cloud had lifted. Another golden ball dispatched.

Bruce Gyngell arrived soon after in a modest Mercedes. I'm sure there was some reason for his visit. Doubtless, Warwick invited him to a pleasant lunch of raclette and *Fendant* and Bruce thought the London to Geneva airfare, a small price for the treat. If so, I wasn't invited, but sensing my post-presentation *Weltschmerz*, Warwick and John invited me to join Bruce for some sight-seeing. Under the cloud by the lake, the view really was magnificent.

"I think it's lifting," Bruce averred with typical certainty and within minutes he was driving us to see a little cottage he was thinking of renting for the next ski season. A modest house, within *langlaufing* distance of the ski runs, proved satisfactory to Bruce and out of reach of anyone without the salary package of a British television CEO.

John sidled up to me as we gazed at the Alps. "Not happy with this morning?" It wasn't a question.

"Humph," I nodded. I had set my expectations high for an enthusiastic response from the marketers, but marketers are naturally practical. "If it works, I like it," my first World Vision boss, David Longe, had sermonised. The beauty of child sponsorship was its simplicity. One sponsor equals one sponsored child, and it allows the inference that what the sponsor gives goes directly to the child. This inference was never entirely true. Even issuing a receipt costs a dollar or two. When all of World Vision's work was in orphanages, the dollar link between sponsor and child had the scent of truth, but we were now twenty years down the track. The field offices were rushing ahead with new practices that were community-based, spread over wider areas, and much more effective in bringing genuine change.

Within a few months, in a small German village, my mood mellowed.

Dorfweil is a little town about 40 kilometres north of Frankfurt. Its houses and public buildings scatter across the gentle slopes of the Weil valley, hence its name Dorfweil, *the village in the Weil.* From my room in the conference centre on the west side of the valley I looked out at summer-green paddocks, a single Lutheran church with cream walls and a typical pointed steeple. The town was an amble down the hill, although I allowed others to inform me.

Here occurred a repeat of the Directors' Conference of Warburton.

Integrity Is The Bedrock Of Reputation

From every corner of the world we came again, two years older, and over two years wiser. Or so it seemed to me. When I saw the conference agenda, you could hear my sigh of relief some distance away. Until Graeme Irvine became President, I could not recall a Partnership level discussion about community development, even though we had projects called "community development" since 1978.

Here I finally sensed a tipping point. Rather boldly, the conference agreed to "A New Vision for Child Sponsorship funded Ministry". At the end of the week, we resolved "World Vision's ministry to children in the 1990s will address the needs and rights of each child in our programs by sponsorship-funded development, in which each sponsor becomes a partner with the family and community on behalf of the child." Here was the statement that allowed further trials, experiments and models of marketing and development practice.

All I had to do, as CEO of World Vision's second biggest funding office, was to persuade my team to get the marketing models right. I felt I could do it, but it would take a much closer working relationship between support and field offices.

Geoff Renner was on my team, responsible for our international programs, and had become an enthusiastic supporter of creating better models for connecting supporters with the field realities. To be fair, his own enthusiasm needed no extra fuelling from me. Having worked at both ends of World Vision, as CEO of the support office in New Zealand and then Vice President for fieldwork in South America, Geoff's enthusiasm was a glass full.

Another resource in this exploration was Ken Tracey. Originally recruited from missionary dental duties in Africa, Ken had been the first VP for Africa. Later he had moved to the international office and had been influential in levering me into the role in Hong Kong. Now, he had agreed to be part of our Australian team. It was great to have this old friend within the house, and I knew he could help us.

Geoff and I travelled to Guatemala to get some insight into the newer models of effective community development led by the impressive field director, Annette de Fortin. I wanted to understand where World Vision's field work was really heading. We learned a lot, mostly by listening. Geoff, still at home in Latin America, knew the right questions to ask, even if sometimes I sensed that his knowledge and experience could sometimes intimidate colleagues. It was certainly possible that the two of us together might appear a pair of heavyweights, but I wanted us to listen and learn, and for me that was easy. I knew so little.

The year 1990 finished well. More than half a million people took part in the *40 Hour Famine*—a record. Child sponsors in Australia passed through 100,000. The *40 Hour Famine* grew by 24% to exceed $7 million for the first time. Total income for the year was also a record—$56 million. And the Board changed my job title from "Executive Director" to "Chief Executive Officer". Some staff soon abbreviated it to "CEO", but I corrected them. I still preferred the name my mother had liked most—Philip.

Almost as the last act of 1990, the Board began looking for fresh blood.

"How many extra members do we think we can absorb at one time?" asked one of the members.

Joan Levett, a member of our Board who resigned at the meeting to take up a staff role in World Vision International, noted the word *absorb*.

"Do we want to *absorb* new members to make them like us," she asked. "Or are we prepared for fresh minds to *change* the Board?"

The consensus agreed that the latter was the case. And so, they put a process into play that would cause me pain. But not for another few years.

* * *

Book 7

The Challenge Of Challenging The Status Quo

42

Give Your Ideas Away, Trust People

I love to give jobs away. I love people who say, "I'll do that." Once I experience that with someone, I have confidence they can repeat the trick. I think this is a key part of effective leadership. Not micromanaging, but showing trust in others.

A CEO's job is complex enough without weighing yourself down with the burden of generating every idea, monitoring every project, checking every timetable. A journalist once asked Stirling Moss, probably the best Formula One driver never to be world champion, whether he checked the mechanical condition of his car before a race.

"No, I check nothing," I remember him answering. "Because, if I started, I would never stop. If I checked just one wheel nut to see if it was tight, I knew I would have to check every wheel nut. Then every tyre pressure, every screw, everything. I decided early, I would trust the mechanics."

But like anyone with a passion for their organisation, I had ideas.

There were things I wanted World Vision to be doing. I could not champion every idea I thought up.

So, if I thought them worth someone following up, I often left a hint or a suggestion. One observant colleague described this habit.

"Philip just leaves ideas lying around," she said, "hoping someone will pick them up." Often someone would pick them up and the idea was no longer mine. It was theirs. They owned it.

Still, there are a few ideas I wished somebody had picked up, but no-one ever did.

There was the childcare idea, for example. I thought there was an opportunity to get into the local childcare business. The market grew as one-income family became more and more passé. There was, for me, a natural fit for World Vision. Children were at the heart of our brand. Why not apply that brand locally? Imagine if there were a visible World Vision Childcare Centre in every suburb and town. Imagine how that would reinforce the message that World Vision cared about children. We did a few sums, but I couldn't stir up enough interest, although quite a few of our working mums relished the idea.

When Pat Cash retired from professional tennis, he helped start a charity, Planet Ark.

"Did you see that Pat Cash is getting into our business now?" I joked with the team over the morning news.

"I think we can stand the competition," someone replied with typical World Vision hubris.

"Why don't we help him?" I asked.

"How?"

"Well, he's going to reinvent the whole back office to manage donations, review suitable projects for support, keep records, follow up supporters. Why should he pay lawyers and administrators big bucks to invent what World Vision already has?"

"And which we could offer to do for a fee," observed Kevin Gray, always getting straight to the heart of the numbers.

"Yes, a little cash flow for World Vision, and at a much lower price than whatever he has to set up by himself."

I was imagining leveraging our investment, delivering child sponsorship and the *40 Hour Famine*. The systems were in place. We could write programs and systems to support the Pat Cash Charity Foundation. Many other famous people with charitable intentions would see the advantage of using our systems. We could provide security against misuse of funds. We could provide a clear audit trail for the authorities.

Two decades down the track one sees fundraising websites using the power of the Internet to sign up support, crowd-fund ideas, provide effortless ways for donors to support a cause with personally branded webpages. If you want to help me support the *40 Hour Famine*, just go to my webpage, give me your credit card, and it's done!

Most of this usefulness is provided by for-profit companies, adding five or ten percent to your donation to recoup their administration costs. You want to give $40. They add $4 as their fee. 100% of your gift goes to the charity (if you ignore the fact that you paid $44). They outsource the admin costs to the web page provider. Brilliant!

What a pity that idea was never picked up. What a shame I didn't follow through on that one.

And here is why.

This week, as I write this, I have signed up online to a World Vision event. The site is not managed by World Vision. As far as I can tell, World Vision has outsourced my participation and fundraising to *everydayhero.com*, a professional fundraising website owned by Blackbaud, "the world's leading cloud software company powering social good." Its market value in 2017 was almost US$5 billion. Located just down the road from where my grandkids lived in Charleston, South Carolina, Blackbaud is an excellent organisation, with world-class products and services for charities. World Vision's use of it is a wise, cost-effective choice.

What a pity Blackbaud is doing what World Vision might have done first.

World Vision was slow to see the coming super-connected world of the Internet. Even in 1990, some of us could see, if dimly, the world of communications was changing. Using our noisy little telephone modems, we were reading our emails at home, and logging onto *Compuserve* to read bulletin boards and get educated by how much uncensored gunk was already littering the online world.

But some ideas were left lying around. Like all splendid ideas, they didn't occur only to one guy on an 8th floor office in South Melbourne. Other people in distant places picked them up. More power and success to them.

I had learned that it's amazing what gets done when I don't care about getting the credit.

* * *

43

Future Surprises, Sometimes You Don't See Them Coming

In mid-1992, I wrote a two-column memo to the Board. With graphs. I was summarising the conversations of the Board about itself, and how that might change.

Much needed to change, but not everything was bath water. Board members were church-attending Christians, although no-one kept tabs. Almost half had lived and worked outside of Australia in relevant occupations. At 12 members it was probably too big. And a bit aging with a median age of 62. We had recruited three of the Board members in the past year, while the other nine had served from nine to 24 years.

The Board went looking for fresher blood, some founding members declared close of innings. Among the fresh faces was an international executive who had drifted into my awareness as CEO of Fairfax, publishers of *The Age* and *The Sydney Morning Herald*. Peter King had assumed control of Fairfax at the behest of its young owner,

Warwick Fairfax, who had borrowed handsomely in 1987 to privatise the company only to see it fail within three years.

During one of our coffee chats at our regular Café Terrace table overlooking the atrium of Melbourne Central, David Jenkin mentioned Peter.

"He's an impressive fellow," he advised, "CEO of Pratt Packaging." Sounded good, I admitted. Big company leadership.

The next few paragraphs filled out the picture. Former CEO of Fairfax. Warwick's man. Both Christian. Connections with the Washington Prayer Breakfast. Former high-level executive with Van Leer, huge Dutch packaging company.

"Is he Dutch?" I asked.

"South African, but he came here with Van Leer about ten years ago and has stayed."

"So, an Aussie now," I commented. "Do you see him as a member of our Board?"

David's response ramped up my interest and, given what happened later, meant I never forgot it.

"Our Board, absolutely," David gushed, "but he could be President of World Vision International."

David's enthusiasm troubled me. He seemed to have covered a lot of distance from possible Australian Board member to President of the whole of our corporate world. But what did I know? Only the gossip about the Fairfax disaster. Perhaps Peter King had been the innocent victim of a callow man's family ambitions. Maybe he had been the only steady hand in a ship heading for cliffs.

Peter joined the World Vision Board in July 1994. *What could go wrong?*

* * *

44

Success Can Hide Tomorrow's Problems

The rest of 1992 through the middle 1995 were busy and exciting years for me. World Vision Australia had grown right through the recession Australia had to have, and continued to grow. By 1995 we were on track to raise $100 million soon. Long way from the $3 million I had thought amazing back in 1978.

A look at my diaries for those years seem to imply superhuman activity. Each day in the office was wall-to-wall meetings. The hour after most staff left at 5pm became the only time to read email. I made Wednesday a work-from-home day to allow me to catch up on reading reports and phone calls. Often these were spent with a four-year-old Richard on my lap. He had long since worked out how to log his name into Microsoft Golf, although the intention of the game seemed to elude him.

I met the Dalai Lama, lots of Canberra politicians and public servants, and tussled amiably with other aid agency leaders as a member of the executive committee of the agency peak body (ACFOA). Most weeks I would be up front for the weekly Big Devos. Most weekends I'd try to get to a Hawthorn game at the MCG. On Sunday I played piano, or sometimes the organ, at Doncaster Church of Christ.

World Vision business took me to Vietnam, Lesotho, South Africa, Somalia, Guatemala, Fiji, Taiwan, Mozambique, Israel, Philippines, South Korea, Kenya, Rwanda, Canada, Costa Rica, Thailand, Zimbabwe, Zambia and India. Board meetings required my presence in Singapore and Hong Kong. Four or five times a year I would be in Los Angeles for meetings at the international office, usually for a week at a time.

By now I had earned the right to Long Service Leave and I took Judy and Richard to Selly Oak, near Birmingham UK, to spend each morning in the library of one college studying and writing a long paper titled "Thinking About Mission". Nobody but me ever read it. During the last week of our stay in Selly Oak I compiled what later became a book, "Journeys to Justice", published in 1995. Judy, Richard and I then drove to Scotland so she could visit her forebears (all long since dead or migrated to Australia).

Late in 1993 I met Peter King for the first time. Oddly, it was in Amsterdam—it just coincided with our travels. The international board had established a review of World Vision's organisational structure. Peter and another consultant, Pat MacMillan, were engaged. We met at the office of World Vision Netherlands and Pat and I enjoyed riffing on ideas of organisational architecture, and sharing my challenges working within the beast that was World Vision. Peter took part very little. I came away wondering what he had gleaned from our discussions and how it would play out in the final report.

One highlight of this time was preparing and co-moderating a conference that brought together all the country leaders of World Vision entities for a week in Tagaytay City, Philippines. Conference theme work occupied most mornings. We gave the afternoons over to the delegates to structure as they wanted. This was novel for World Vision conferences, which were usually tightly structured to serve agendas that did not always satisfy those attending. It worked brilliantly. Groups popped up around things that needed airing. Once satisfied, there was time for play or sight-seeing. From that time since, I have always included large slabs of *structure-yourself* time in conferences.

Success Can Hide Tomorrow's Problems

It sounds like I was never in the office, but even in the busy-ness of 1994 I was in town and in the office much more than not. Presence matters, but the quality of presence matters more. I usually took lunch in the staff lunchroom and tried to arrive early enough to get a seat at the card game. And I had long learned the art of MBWA—Managing By Wandering About. I'm naturally introverted. I'm content with working at my computer or engaging in solo pursuits like cycling or learning to fly. But just because that's home for my personality doesn't mean I have to live there. Your body may be right-handed, but that ought not prevent you from using your left.

Meanwhile, an incurable dissatisfaction niggled. Our Vision Challenge and Core Values process seemed to have had a merely superficial impact on the organisation's culture. We paid lip-service to the core values, but I observed, too often, that the way we behaved was at odds with what we said.

Our Core Values were extensively worked out in the late 1980s. It involved all of World Vision. These six belief statements emerged:

> *We are Christian*
> *We value people*
> *We are partners*
> *We are committed to the poor*
> *We are stewards*
> *We are responsive*

The international council adopted these just before I accepted the role of CEO of World Vision Australia.

Four years on, a colleague, John Steward, asked me why so many of us were dubious about the significance of the core values. John offered to invite staff to meet with him to talk about it.

On 25th June 1993 53 staff responded to his invitation. Ten sent apologies, and a further ten sent messages of support after the meeting. One manager reported that none of his department would be at the meeting because every member feared repercussions if they came.

The group of 53 produced twelve typewritten pages of mostly negative concerns. This became their vision, under John's leadership, of what they wanted to move beyond. Reporting back, John said, "our vision was a WVA where there would be no basis for such negative feeling because these core values were being consciously and consistently applied. We would resolve problems with openness and maturity. We saw this would require radical change. We must change ourselves first." Here were principles of community development John had learned at the sharp end of World Vision's work.

The group dwindled to fifteen faithfuls, meeting on the second Thursday of each month and sometimes when there was an urgent issue. It got a name—The Campaign to Conserve the Core Values of World Vision Australia. I joined with Merilyn Hill, our HR Manager, to openly support the group which helped to allay fears of some. The CCCV became a forum in which they could discuss behavioural issues outside of the hierarchy. Often, they met simply to pray. More often than not, matters prayed for were resolved. The group was laying the groundwork for a vision of a new World Vision.

* * *

45

If You're Dissatisfied, Don't Just Sit There, Do Something

The year 1995, it began well. Manfred Grellert, Vice President for Latin America, invited me to attend the conference of his country leaders. We worked, mostly in Spanish, which is my sixth language behind English, German, Cantonese, French and Korean. Since I can only say "Hello" and "Thank-you" in most of these, I badly needed an interpreter. I never knew her name, but she stayed close and whispered in my ear. This sounds romantic but she was at the back of the room, and I was wearing a headset. I expanded my Spanish vastly during the week in Costa Rica, adding "*café con leche*" and "*obrigado*", until the Brazilians told me the latter was actually Portuguese.

Something else happened under the Costa Rica skies. I realised I was drifting. I had finished 6 years as CEO. Yet I felt I had not yet done everything the organisation required. My time with the Latin team of smart, deep thinking, men and women leaders reminded me of my calling. More than that, it was as if I got shot with some Latino adrenaline.

I expressed my frustrations in a fax home to Judy:

> The conference has been the usual mixed bag for me. I have this vision of an organisation that organises itself around the basic management unit of the project and the people (donors) supporting the project. Very decentralised. This has been my vision for over ten years. While I see some progress towards this, it is VERY slow. Often people see problems with something, usually a system that causes unintended consequences, and I am sure I know the solution is in the fundamentals about how we organise and manage, but they keep trying to fix the system. The problem is elsewhere. For example, we have set up yet another international task force. This time to "define overhead" so that there can be "clear international guidelines". Most people think this is a splendid idea. But it isn't. It's like trying to design a bus system for the world from an office high in the Empire State Building. It would never work. The only way to do it, is to design a small bus system in each suburb, then link them together in some form of network. It seems so obvious to me, but it requires a paradigm shift, and this is most difficult. We like what we know and will do handstands to avoid change. 'Twas ever thus.

* * *

Towards the end of the conference, Manfred approached me.

"Philip, you are the most senior person here," he said, "would you prepare a summary statement to share with the team?"

"Most senior person here?" I objected. "Surely, Manfred, that is you." He was older than me and this was his turf. I was just a visitor.

"But I am always here," he said. I wasn't sure that answer made any sense.

The "most senior." I disliked the label. I was 47. I was too young to be "the most senior". I could still play volleyball with the best Latin America could offer, if not nearly as well. I had not earned this title.

It was an odd appellation to bear. Perhaps I could envisage a future World Vision in which such labels did not exist.

Nevertheless, I prayed and thought about what I might say to these wonderful colleagues. It was this:

"I believe:
- in God's faithfulness.
- in God's mission in the world. He acts in the world. God is working his purpose out as year succeeds to year.
- that God invites us to join him in his mission. It is a gracious invitation. We have done nothing to deserve it. And there is nothing we can do, to deserve it.
- God does not really need us to participate in his mission. I must believe that, since I believe God is all-powerful. Yet, despite his power and his strength, God likes us, he likes me, enough to want us to take part in his mission with him.
- that World Vision is part of God's mission in the world.
- that there is a lot of wisdom in World Vision, sufficient wisdom for any task to which God calls us.
- that World Vision's wisdom does not reside in one person's head, nor in one place, nor in one structure. Everyone has wisdom. And everyone has some wisdom that someone else does not have.
- that we are inventing a new World Vision in which we can tap this vast reservoir of wisdom.
- that the world is changing fast. Too fast. In my country, I am told that 70% of the jobs we shall do in the year 2010 have not yet been invented. How can I plan for a world which has not yet been invented?
- that a fast-changing world requires our strategic planning to be about releasing the wisdom of the organisation to apply itself in real time to real day to day problems, rather than writing long range plans that gather dust.
- that leadership will be more about empowering staff to act, than about telling them what to do.
- that leadership will be more about holding people accountable for results, than about checking whether they are doing things right.

- that leadership will be more about alignment with vision and values, than about adherence to policies and procedures.
- that success comes from obedience to God.
- that obedience means living transcendentally in the mundane and commonplace things of life.
- that lunch can be as transcendental as liturgy; that accounting can be as transcendental as communion; that work can be worship.
- that we are on the right track.
- that God is working his purpose out in World Vision.
- that God's timing for resolution of these issues may not be the same as ours. I am comfortable with this in my mind, if sometimes frustrated by this in my spirit. I note that we also discussed some issues discussed here, in a conference involving me and Manfred in Salvador, Bahia, Brazil in 1982. God has not felt World Vision is ready yet for some of his answers. Patience is a virtue.
- all virtue comes from God. Therefore, I am patient."

But my spirit was *not* patient. I left Costa Rica with an elevated heartbeat. I had waited long enough. Now was the moment to stop dreaming of what could be. It was time to fix my mind on making it happen. *Now we must accelerate.*

When Formula 1 world champion, Sir Lewis Hamilton, comes to a corner, he selects a point before the apex to push the accelerator. When surfing world champion, Stephanie Gilmore, approaches a wave, she selects a point before the crest to paddle harder. When casual cyclist, Philip Hunt, saw the 100-metre false flat at the top of Lavers Hill he pedalled harder. The more momentum you carry as gravity becomes your friend, the easier and faster is the way forward.

Or, the time to push for organisational change is when everything is going well. At such a time, there is motivation and mood to push ahead while we are strong.

Perhaps the bard William Shakespeare expressed the organisational implications best in a speech he wrote for Brutus:

If You're Dissatisfied, Don't Just Sit There, Do Something

> *There is a tide in the affairs of men,*
> *Which, taken at the flood, leads on to fortune;*
> *Omitted, all the voyage of their life*
> *Is bound in shallows and in miseries.*
> *On such a full sea are we now afloat,*
> *And we must take the current when it serves,*
> *Or lose our ventures.*[2]

Looking over the Gulf of Mexico from seat 31D on flight AA964 from San Jose, the CEO of World Vision Australia determined that 28th January 1995 was such a moment to pedal harder.

And I knew where to begin.

* * *

---

[2] William Shakespeare, Julius Caesar, Act 4, Scene 3, 218—224.

46

Listen To The Next Generation. It's Their Future, Not Yours

I am a Baby Boomer. Born in 1948. A good proportion of World Vision staff were Gen X. I decided to throw the challenge to them.

By some process, democratic or otherwise, I invited six staff members and one Board member who had one thing in common. They were all under 35 years of age. I called them the "2013 Commission". They were four women and three men.

I invited them with the comment that 70% of the jobs in the year 2010 had not been invented yet. Gen X were children when colour television arrived in their homes. By 1994 they had matured with the digital world. Most owned computers. A few had a mobile phone and a Walkman. Few had any idea of the social media cataclysm a mere decade ahead.

We were in a time of sudden and discontinuous change. De Klerk in South Africa had suddenly set Nelson Mandela free. Northern Ireland seemed to be heading for peace. There were glimmers (soon extinguished) of change in Palestine.

Why 2013?

"Because," I said, "that's the year I will be 65 and probably should retire from World Vision."

"In the year 2013 it will not matter whether the organisation suits me, since I shall leave it. It will matter to you. You will still be here (or others like you). It is important, as I think about where World Vision Australia is going, that I listen to younger people about the organisation you want to create. If I know where you want to go, I can try to make sure you recognise the place when we get there.

"Why you? Because you are 35 or under, and I think you have some ability to think freely about the future.

"What do I want you to do? To develop a vision of the World Vision Australia you would like to see in the year 2013.

"How will you do that? That's up to you."

The outcome was everything I hoped for and more. The group not only had brilliant ideas but were thrilling in presentation. No 33-page memo for them. Instead, they took over the entire building and transported us all into the year 2013.

I wish I had a video to show you because most of the details have faded from memory. Except for one ultra-delight.

As the 2013 Tour Guide shuffled my small group towards my office, I noted it had a sign on the door. "Childcare." Inside, the office chairs and table were gone. Spread out on the floor, a half dozen of our young Mums sat playing with their toddlers. They had converted my office into a Childcare facility.

This touched my heart more than they could know. Sometimes one wonders if anyone is listening. Or, if anything sinks in. Here was proof positive.

Yes, the office of 2013 ought to have a Childcare facility. Aren't we in the business of caring for kids? Isn't that what our biggest program is about? Why would we not want to care for the kids of our staff in this beautiful way? These young mums were living out a belief about who we wanted to be. Core values demonstrated in action.

* * *

47

Transfer Or Transform Is The Core Issue

I wrote a case study during my MBA studies about how to change an organisation. I based it on an idea I read somewhere, that organisations are *frozen* and need to be *melted* before we can reshape them. The analogy was good, but easier to say than to do.

I wanted to change World Vision, beginning in Australia. That's all I was responsible for, but it would be nice if we could model something globally. If that were the case, others would be on their own to pick up the ideas. I had no desire to be international President.

I had been on a journey since 1976. I knew where World Vision had been, and I thought I knew where it needed to go. I was neither alone, nor the deepest thinker. I had settled my ideas for change by 1991. At a conference in Azusa, California, I sensed a shift. I wanted to test our readiness to think afresh. I began with the question I had asked back in Chapter 42.

"Are we a transfer or a transform organisation?"

I told the assembled World Vision colleagues that I thought *transfer* best described who we had been, but that *transform* best described where we were going. There seemed to be some interest in the room, so I pressed the advantage.

"The answer to the question has implications for organisational design," I suggested. The implications then gushed out of me like a man with two heads:

What would be the organisation's strategy, its common task, the one thing that everyone contributes to?

In a transfer organisation the strategy would be to transfer resources from the rich to the poor.

In a transform organisation the strategy would empower people so that individuals and community lives would be transformed in ways that bring the Kingdom of God alive.

What's the goal of the organisation?

For the transfer organisation, let's get the money transferred from A to B quickly and cheaply.

For the transform organisation, let's see people changed from their present conditions to full lives in all its dimensions.

What would success look like?

Transfer organisations would adhere to budget. If it came in on time and on budget, it's a success. How many wells were dug? What did it cost?

Transform organisations would want to see signs of the Kingdom, love, joy, peace, patience, kindness, faithfulness, gentleness and self-control. What impact did it have on people?

What kind of structure would accomplish this strategy?

The structures might look similar in each. The differences would lie in power. A transfer organisation would have a traditional hierarchy of authority. There may be participative processes, but the boss will be the one with whom the buck stops.

Relationships in a transform organisation would be more autonomous and negotiated. At the centre would remain the right to arbitrate on matters of principle. What those matters of principle are, would be a critical strategic question.

> *What would be the things, we would give attention to at head office and when we met in corporate forums?*

A transfer organisation would meet around finances, planning and reporting. How are we doing in Bangladesh? Fine. Great audit.

A transform organisation would meet around people and values. What kind of person are we looking for to be the new Field Director in Bangladesh? Let's agree on the right person with the right heart.

> *What would be the concerns we would distribute away from the centre, allowing managers to develop their own standards and methods?*

In a transfer organisation you would find mission, vision, values and paradigms worked out differently in every location.

In a transform organisation you would find financial systems, budgets and planning, locally developed to fit the need.

> *What would be the dominant management tool used to control our people?*

In a transfer organisation it is the budget. You would have a centrally controlled and managed audit team that went round the world inspecting. Auditors and accountants would be kings.

In a transform organisation, you would have centralised agreements on how subsidiary organisations adhered to the vision and values. A consistent, centrally managed vision and values audit process. Peer reviewers and culture evangelists would be kings.

There was a lot more of this. I sketched it out on the whiteboard.

For about 30 minutes there was a buzz of conversation. I looked around the room. I felt I could read the faces. A few colleagues clearly thought I was on another planet. Another few seemed to get it right away. They spoke out with enthusiasm and it warmed my heart. In between, there was shoulder shrugging. The international organisation was not ready.

Perhaps the Australian organisation was.

* * *

48

Don't Lose The Wonder

Just before Christmas 1994, I got back from a week in Seoul and Hong Kong. I know it must seem ungrateful and perhaps unbelievable, but I found most international trips boring. This was the 5th or 6th time I had been to Seoul. And I had been to Hong Kong so many times, people in the street would say *Jou San* to me. When you travel for business, rather than pleasure, a jumbo jet soon becomes just another big bus in the sky.

I wouldn't say I found the work boring. As usual, it was such a pleasure to be with World Vision people. Here, 13 other members of Asian World Vision Boards. 14 of us praying the Lord's Prayer in our mother tongues, 13 distinct languages.

As usual, the work was interesting and fulfilling, but the travelling was boring. I regret to say it had become commonplace for me, and I had become rather blasé about this so-called jet-setting.

When I got back, our young son Richard immediately wanted

to go down to the schoolyard to throw the frisbee and ride his bike. Dutifully, I went with him. Judy said, "You're a good Dad," more to remind me about what "good Dads" do, than what I felt in my spirit.

I sat down on a bench in the shade of an avenue of cypress trees and looked across the playground to Mount Dandenong, which is a backdrop to where we lived in Melbourne. Richard wanted to go riding down the hill. I assured him he could, and that I would be right here on the seat.

"If I don't come back, you'll come and look for me?" Richard asked. And I assured him indeed I would.

He rode off, bouncing over the rough ground and obviously enjoying the thrill of speed and exploring the limits of his control.

In a minute he turned a corner and was out of sight. In less than a minute more he was back, red in the face and beaming with excitement. "I went right over to the Grade 5 area," he said, "further than I've ever been before!" David Livingstone, finding Victoria Falls, could not have been more excited.

It struck me how blasé I had become about the wonders of the world. The Grade 5 area is a wonder to those who are going through the wonder years. But much of life is a wonder, and too many of us have forgotten how to be awe-struck.

That those big Boeings actually fly is a routine, everyday awesome event. The rich variety and the stunning diversity of human culture and experience is an everyday, ordinary wonder. These are things about which a fully human person ought not to lose a sense of wonder and amazement.

* * *

49

Board Development Is A Continuous And Intensive Process

The Board of World Vision Australia numbered 15 persons. It had grown large by neglect, but it was an impressive group of people. One could hardly say those people were not eminent and suitable. Read their CVs and it would be churlish to be unimpressed.

There were just *too many* of them.

I was no expert on Boards. Yes, I had created and chaired the World Vision Boards in Hong Kong and Singapore, but these were not yet fully responsible Boards. When, in 1995, the Hong Kong Board had grown to a half dozen local, well-connected and talented eminences, I resigned the chair and, soon after, my seat on the Board.

There is, I have discovered, an ideal size for an effective Board. Seven is the magic number. It has to be an odd number, because even numbers result in 50/50 votes. Giving a casting vote to the chair is often the solution, unfairly making the chair more powerful than any other Board member.

The World Vision board met four times a year. It had members from every mainland State. (Sorry Tasmania!) It met for a day and a half each time. No-one got paid, but we had to feed everyone, and the interstaters came by plane and normally required a hotel room. It was expensive.

But worse, it was too big to work. Even meeting for a day and a half did not permit fifteen people to all get a say. Either topics ran on for hours, while other matters queued up, or a half dozen speakers dominated and everyone else nodded or shrugged their shoulders. It occurred to me we'd be better off just letting that half dozen talkers be the Board and retire the rest.

In a way, that had happened. A board executive of, wait for it, *seven* people met between regular Board meetings. It got things done, usually without provoking hours of later discussions in the big meeting. Why not just let them be the Board? No-one, not even me, was asking.

The other issue, when it later came, was a complete surprise. David Jenkin, who had appointed, mentored and corrected me, and with whom I shared so many similar dreams for our organisation, was approaching a breaking point. He had been in poor health through the latter part of 1994 but now seemed back in robustness. Lois, David's wife, needed a kidney transplant. Finding the right donor was worryingly slow. It was clear this dilemma was David's constant companion. In the meantime, David was about to become chair of the international Board and had been deeply engaged, along with Peter King, in the review of the international organisation.

Something had to give, and I just did not see it coming.

A third potential fly in the governance ointment was the relative inexperience of the newer Board members. One-third of the Board had been with us less than two years. They critically lacked experience of World Vision itself, which was hardly their fault.

I would often say, not really in jest, that the best thing we could do for new donors was to send a free airline ticket to a World Vision project with the receipt for their first donation. When donors visited a project in Kenya, Thailand, the Philippines or Ecuador, we had 'em for life.

When you meet the people who work in World Vision projects, when you meet the people in the community, when you see what happens, what a difference World Vision is making in their lives—only then do you understand that it's *not* about fundraising and transferring dollars. Then you understand it is about people and their future.

From this distant point of view, I realise we did nothing to help our new Board members enjoy this essential revelation. Instead, they approached World Vision with what they saw reflected off our surface. $90 million income. 300 staff. Two storey bespoke building in Burwood East. Modern business systems. A CEO with an MBA.

But this was not World Vision. This was just the sheen reflecting off a deep well of love, mercy and a commitment to rescue, empowerment and human development. We had no Board induction process that exposed Board members effectively to the depths of this reality. One could talk about it, and we did. But our messages were diluted or misheard, by the reality that Board members only brushed against the organisation in its Melbourne office four or five times a year.

Some years later, when my World Vision journey had taken me to Eastern Europe and the Middle East, I discovered that time heals and educates. I met some of these then-new Board members after they had learned what we were all about. The changes were written in words that sprang from re-educated hearts.

I too, had been naïve about World Vision when I joined in the 1970s, but I could do little damage from my lowly place as the organisational copywriter. In 1995 we were embarking on a revolution and we had not prepared some of our cadre.

A change in the weather approached. One issue brought it into focus. *Remuneration.*

We paid our staff by comparing each position to external salary data and then setting salaries at the lowest quartile. What that meant was that, for any position in World Vision, the salary would be at the point where 75% of people doing that job out there in the world were paid more. Or 25% were paid less.

This market-based process had been in place before I became CEO. I thought it was fair and appropriately conservative for a charity. Suddenly, unfamiliar voices on the Board were asking how we justified paying Philip Hunt $135,000 a year.

That was a very good salary in the mid-90s. Our policy argued, if it could speak for itself, that World Vision paid the CEO less than three-quarters of CEOs doing similar jobs in similar size organisations. World

Vision was a $90 million a year operation with 385 staff. I knew that the CEO of CARE Australia was on $120,000 in an organisation half our size but growing fast. The CEO of Community Aid Abroad (soon to be OXFAM) took home about $50,000 in an organisation one-fifth the size of World Vision Australia. Just the same, the minimum wage was around $18,000 a year, and average annual earnings were in the low $30s.

I agreed that it was perfectly reasonable for the Board to review our remuneration policy. It had not done so for some years. It was time. The Board appointed a Remuneration Task Force that contained no staff. They did not seem to be interested in understanding the remuneration process already in place. Unwelcome inferences punctuated their comments.

The Task Force asked for a policy that was "transparent and open to public scrutiny" without observing that the existing policy was already a public document. There was no secret about how World Vision established its salaries. People often asked questions about salaries and we readily explained our approach. And then, despite this request for openness, the Board asked for the doors to be closed during the discussion of a paper unnecessarily branded "Private and Confidential" on every page.

One speaker suggested that I believed morale to be a matter of salary alone. This was so wrong an inference as to leave me despairing that I could be so misunderstood. Salary so low that it represents injustice may be a factor in low morale, but I knew that most people came to work at World Vision not for the money, but because of the *meaning* they got from their jobs.

The commentary was uncomfortable and loaded, maybe unintentionally, with negative inferences. I had always accepted my pay without question or request. No, that's not right. One time, when we were in Hong Kong, I asked my boss to *reduce* my salary because the exchange rates had moved the numbers too much in my favour beyond what I had accepted on appointment. The boss reduced my salary and wrote back, "I have never been asked this request in my entire managerial life!" I had never once asked for a pay rise in two decades with World Vision, and the previous year I had foregone the pay rise offered.

I could not remain silent as I read the suggestion that "World

Vision Australia had been caught up in the spirit of the greedy 80s." Perhaps I reacted rather too loudly, pointing out that even though World Vision's income grew at 18% per year, our salaries remained benchmarked to external market realities. We did not measure ourselves against ourselves.

Ironically, the Task Force proposed following the policy of World Vision Canada, which I heartily endorsed, since they had based their policy on ours—something I pointed out. When the revised policy was implemented a few months later, all the senior people got a raise—something I didn't point out. But I wondered *what all the fuss was about.*

* * *

50

Search The Future, Recognise What You Know

In February 1995, a fascinating three-day search took place. It involved staff from different corners, Board members, people from agencies outside of World Vision Australia (often considered competitors) and others. The idea for a "Future Search Conference" had not been mine. My colleagues, Merilyn Hill and Greg Thompson introduced me to it, and then organised it. It was a time of rich learning. A sense of direction emerged from what we already knew. Our inherent knowledge became the basis for thinking about, dreaming about and planning for the future.

There was merely one downside. Only a few Board members were available. Newer Board members, who now comprised about a third of our mammoth 15-person Board, were notably absent. I wasn't expecting every Board member to attend for three complete days. Board members are busy by definition and some lived interstate, but I had hoped that most would drop by for a half a day, or a few hours.

I was not deterred. The Board had already given us a framework for change. They had asked me to go ahead in their recent meeting. I doubt it crossed my mind that I had less than their full support.

A month later a group of about twenty staff met and worked on the vision statement and four strategic objectives inherited from the Board. Looking back on the work by so many staff, I am in awe of its quality. Hardly any issue went untouched, nor failed to be commented upon with a look to the future. A draft strategic plan emerged from this group and I circulated it to the Board, inviting their feedback.

I reported that the Future Search process had created a consensus on the need for change—the first goal of unfreezing the organisation. I noted some natural reluctance to define that change in practical ways, but I felt there was enthusiasm building which would yield good fruit. In my CEO report to the May Board, I noted, "Board involvement has been practically difficult, and we need to compensate for this. I hope we can give substantial time to the process at the Board retreat."

* * *

51

Give Accountability To People, Not Teams

Politicians rarely invite one to a meeting. Usually, it's the other way round, and it's not always good news when they do. In the middle of 1995, I got an urgent message to meet with Gordon Bilney, the Minister for Development Cooperation. The invitation was not merely for me, but to all agency heads. Its purpose was "to discuss draft Terms of Reference for a Code of Practice Advisory Committee."

Gordon wanted to create a "Code of Practice for NGDOs", by which he meant Non-Government Development Organisations. Oh good. One more clumsy abbreviation. But wait. There was more.

The Committee would enforce the Code. The Government would expect compliance from all agencies and, get this, "compliance would be linked to tax deductibility and access to Government funding." Hello, *Big Stick*.

Within a week I was on the early flight to Canberra with my colleague, Ian Curtis, who was responsible for our relations with the Government. His work was yielding millions of dollars a year in funding for World Vision projects.

There were two things going on in the background. One good and one bad.

The good one which Gordon Bilney knew about, was the work that ACFOA, the agency peak body, was almost finished in strengthening its Code of Ethics which required all member agencies to comply with. We wondered why a CPAC (a Code of Practice Advisory Committee) wasn't plainly redundant.

The bad thing involved CARE Australia and the *Sunday* program. Malcolm Fraser, chair of CARE, takes up the story.

> "On 26 May 1995, Channel Nine's Sunday *program devoted an episode to CARE Australia in which ... (things) ... were cast in the worst possible light. It was said that CARE Australia had 'mismanaged vital aid projects ... misused funds and ... deceived the Australian public, the Australian Government and the United Nations.*
>
> *"Added to this were entirely fictitious allegations that rice had been used to pay bribes and that CARE Australia had 'double dipped' by applying for funding for the same project from two sources."*[3]

You might presume there is a back story here, and you would be right. In November of the previous year, CARE Australia's activities had been quietly and forensically audited at the request of Gordon Bilney, the Minister responsible for Australia's government aid program. "All was not as it should have been," says Malcolm Fraser.

To their credit, CARE Australia hid nothing, corrected their accounting, and returned a little over $200,000 to the government which they had used in a way not permitted under their contract with the government. A *Trucks for Bosnia* campaign also drew attention as, by the time they raised the funds, there were better ways to transport the aid. No trucks were bought.

The process was exemplary of government accountability. I

---
3   Malcolm Fraser and Margaret Simons, *Malcolm Fraser: The Political Memoirs*, The Miegunyah Press, 2015, p. 681.

thought it showed that the system worked. There are rules. There are ways of ensuring the rules are not broken. There are consequences and remedies if they are.

CARE Australia lay the problems at the feet of too rapid growth in its early years. To me, this was a reasonable defence. Or, at least, grounds for compensation, forgiveness and organisational learning. I didn't like it when people made mistakes. But I wanted to allow anyone to make a mistake once. That's how people learn. Organisations, too. Of course, if you make the same mistake twice, we need to have a serious chat.

I thought the government had properly handled the problem and the story would go no further. But, then, television and the *Sunday* program.

"Donations plummeted," says Malcolm Fraser. CARE Australia considered closing down, but survived.

And then, without a word about CARE or the *Sunday* program, our presence was demanded in Canberra.

We were seated around tables arranged in a big square. I chose a place with my back to a window. Never sit facing the light if you need to see your opponent's eyes. Jim Carlton, who had retired from political life to become the CEO of Australian Red Cross, slipped in beside me. Ian pulled a chair up behind so he could whisper condemnations in my ear. Ian was never a fan of Labor governments, whereas I was just never a fan of politics.

Gordon arrived with the staff and the senior people from AIDAB (the government aid agency) and made his introductory remarks. I don't recall any of the meeting except my rising anger at the audacity of calling us all to Canberra, at the expense of our own agencies, to be schooled in responsibilities of which we were well aware. And furthermore, responsibilities we complied with and could demonstrate.

"I'm sorry," I said. I think I may have interrupted someone who was already speaking.

"I'm sorry, but this is wrong. It is not fair. I feel like I am back in grade 5 and the whole class is being kept in because one pupil has been naughty."

I took a breath, thinking others might jump in, but the only sound was the air-conditioning.

"You don't have a problem with most of the people in the room," I continued. "You have a problem with one agency, and it is with them you should deal, and let the rest of us get back to work."

Whatever happened after that, we never saw a Code of Practice Advisory Committee.

* * *

Book 8

The Edges Fray

52

It's Going Well, But...

In the first half of 1995, I kept seeing glimmers of change. Occasionally there would be a flash of hope.

David Jenkin circulated two extracts from the Harvard Business Review to Board members. The articles argued for major time commitments from non-executive Board members. All of our Board members were non-executive.

The 2013 Commission had people talking in corridors. And toilets—it never failed to surprise me how much stuff got done while staff washed their hands.

The Board revised the job description for the CEO, confirming my role as chief advisor to the Board and the authorised spokesperson for World Vision "on all matters except those reserved to the Board Chair." There was no list of matters reserved for the Board Chair. David had never sought to be the organisation's spokesperson, and I assumed that would continue.

I wrote a paper on Federalism. The following quotes caused a lively discussion in the management team.

> *Federalism is a very different, and very uncomfortable way of thinking about organisations. It is messy, untidy, and always a little out of control. Its only justification is that there is no real alternative in a complicated world. No one person, or group, or executive, is so all-wise and so all-sensitive to balance the paradoxes on their own, or run the place from the centre, even if people were prepared to allow them.*

> *The centre's role is to orchestrate the broad strategic vision, develop the shared administrative and organisational infrastructure, and create the cultural glue which can create synergies.*

On the 20th April, I updated staff through my regular Trellis newsletter:

> Last week we had another step in the Future Search process. Almost 100 staff were criticising, clarifying, contributing.
>
> Among the things we agreed about:
>
> - World Vision Australia is somewhere near the top of our present Sigmoid curve (if you don't know what a Sigmoid curve is, ask someone).
> - things need to change.
> - the present language of the "Strategic Plan" is unclear (one person described it as "gobbledygook").
> - There's not enough action in the plan yet.
>
> What is the next step?
>
> We've talked and learned so much. And I've talked, listened and learned with you. It is my turn to work

It's Going Well, But...

on our strategic plan myself. I'll be spending much of next week rewriting the plan, making it easier to read and understand, and putting more action into it.

Then we shall have Strategic Plan number 3. After a week for comment, I shall present this to the Board. They have an important part to play in ensuring that we have done good work, and that it is the right work.

That means that by the end of May we should have some challenging stuff to get on with.

Then we can do it.

* * *

Alongside all this great work, our HR colleagues had led us through a review of the role of women in the organisation. For this we had engaged Fay Marles, former Commissioner for Equal Opportunity in Victoria. Her report bristled with things to change in our attitudes to and support for women. I was a learner and an enthusiast. One outcome, not the least by any means, was to purchase a breast pump which resulted in an award from the Nursing Mothers Association.

I was confident and in high spirits. It seemed there was a swell of movement towards something new and exciting that would keep me and the team busy for another decade at least.

* * *

53

Liminal Work Towards A New Organisation

Between the May Board meeting and the next one in August, every meeting room seemed occupied. Busy bees working through the possibilities of the Next Curve. I had little to do apart from answer the occasional question, or react to some outlandish, but thrilling, ideas. In parallel, I listed twenty issues that the Board had raised and assigned responsibilities to work on them.

Three staff groups met around three topics. The question before us was what kind of organisation structure best suited the World Vision we wanted. I did not take part directly but waited for their wisdom.

Group 1 examined organising around our two customers and how we could group them by program. A second group looked at organising by location. A third group explored organising around customer type. There was a collaborative sharing of papers that coalesced in an easy majority around customer-focussed business units.

This became a structure of six new strategic business units that a

General Manager would lead. We would design each to serve one group of customers—existing supporters, major supporters, new supporters, groups (church, staff groups, clubs), corporations, government and multilateral organisations, supported by four staff groups. Job descriptions for the leaders of each of these new units were already in draft form.

I announced all this to the staff at Big Devos. I just needed to navigate the change process through the August Board meeting later that week.

I had not had a formal performance appraisal during my time under David Jenkin's chairing. To be fair, every morning coffee meeting with David was part appraisal. He never held back from questioning and advising.

As David moved into the international arena more and more, we found ourselves often in the same room. Sometimes even arguing the opposite. There was never rancour in international meetings. Or, at least, it was kept in check; but I was often weary of trudging the same path for change and seeing no actual change.

"You were surprisingly quiet in the meetings last week," David said to me one time we were meeting at our usual spot just a few days after landing from the same meeting in Los Angeles.

"Yeah, I'm tired of getting nowhere," I confessed. "I just didn't feel I had the energy to keep walking the arguments through the quicksand."

"Well, you must," he said with surprising force. "You can't just say you don't have the energy. This is your job. I don't care if it's hard work. It's *your* work."

He was right. I never forgot the rebuke. Sometimes a mentor needs to speak plainly.

With Peter King on the board came the suggestion that there be a formal performance appraisal of the CEO. It may not have been Peter's suggestion. I don't recall, but it was Peter who was nominated to tell me the truth.

No-one was more surprised than I to find the process, and Peter's part in it, professionally handled and helpful. Perhaps I had been hasty in forming a judgement.

From time to time, the Head of Business and Corporate Development at BHP, Russell Fynmore, had been kind enough to share substantial donations with World Vision from that company's vast wealth.

"I want to introduce you to some other CEOs," he said on the phone. It was a compliment that he included me with the CEOs he had in mind.

A few weeks later I met this impressive group of "other CEOs". I sat with the heads of ALCOA, Woodside Petroleum, Comalco and the Gas and Fuel Corporation. I was seriously out of my league, but I like to think they didn't notice.

The opportunity was there for me to talk about World Vision. Buoyed up by what I was trying to create back at 1 Vision Drive, I made a wild claim.

"I see World Vision in the future as a billion-dollar organisation," I said. I think everyone was smiling at this audacity. But I wanted to assure them I was serious.

"Poverty is not an economic problem," I said, walking down a now familiar rhetorical path. "The world has more money than the job requires."

"It's not even a management problem. We know how the job can be done. We just have to scale it up. If we're going to get the job done, it will take some substantial organisations to do it. I want World Vision Australia to be one of them."

I concluded with a cheeky invitation.

"I hope I see the day when any of you would think of coming to World Vision as chief executive as a most natural and significant career step."

* * *

54

Chickens Do Come Home To Roost

Under the chairmanship of Professor Ian Breward, the Board met for its August meeting. We started with a repeat of the 2013 Commission's presentation. We walked the Board around the building as the 2013 Commission described the future. The staff were brilliant. The process clever, entertaining and informative. The Board enjoyed it. I commented later that I had never seen Ian Breward, who had a somewhat melancholic reputation, smiling so much and for so long. It was the perfect way to talk about the future, because it had revealed the future.

Then it got hard. Followed by difficult. And soon, *impossible*.

First item on the agenda, Proposals for Organisational Change. The early questioning was unremarkable. Some wanted something explained. A clarification asked for. Information requested for reassurance. This felt normal and good. But then there was a pivotal moment. The talk shifted to the significance of what was being proposed. Surprise emerged at the edges of questions. It was as if the Board was saying, "You're doing *what*?"—although no-one quite put it that way.

I looked at the faces around the table. Perhaps half of them looked like they realised they were suddenly facing decisions for which they were unprepared. There was anxiety in the room. There was a slab of it in my gut.

David Jenkin and Bruce Redpath talked to support moving towards a business unit approach. There seemed little opposition to this key proposal. Oddly, David and Bruce seemed to argue the logical opposites. Bruce sticking to his own experience of decentralising geographically, while David admired the customer focus which implied different sized business units.

The next turn in the conversation was "whether the Board has enough information to make decisions." At that moment, I knew we were in trouble. Because the Board clearly did not have enough information. I had known this from my first revolutionary appeal a year earlier. I saw it now fully clear for the first time. We had not engaged the Board enough. Whose fault was that?

"At our meeting last November…," I began a rescue attempt. Our meeting. I wanted to say *your* meeting. I wanted to disown the problem. I wanted them to see it was their problem, not mine. But I didn't want a confrontation. I wanted us all to be on the same side.

"At our meeting last November, I specifically asked the Board's direction about its level of involvement in this change process. You'll remember. It was one of the questions on the overhead. I asked you…" Yes, *you*. "I asked the Board to establish policy and standards to guide this process. It was on our agenda. I asked you to decide and tell me how you wanted to be involved." I took a breath. No-one jumped in. A *Point of No Return* skated quietly by.

Was it even possible for the Board to be now adequately engaged in the momentum for change? I had created that moment for them almost a year ago. Why should they be surprised now to find they had insufficient information to make decisions? Through their inaction they had delegated those decisions. Those decisions had already been made—by the people who turned up.

"You were very firm in your direction to me," I reminded. I tried to keep my tone even. "You said, 'Get on with it,' and, 'Stop talking and make this happen.' That's what you said to me. So, I've done what you asked. I have delivered an organisational change plan that we can roll out tomorrow."

I was doing what they asked, and I had kept them informed on the way, and they had not delivered their part. When I had reported progress, the only response I got was advice to slash costs, sack staff and slash and burn. I now realise that this had been, in the minds of its proponents, their strategic response—Business Process Re-engineering, salary caps, cost cuts. But we were trying to create a new innovating organisation, not create efficiencies in an old business-as-usual one. The Board had not been of one mind. So, they let the process run. Some Board members took part. Others were absent. Now there were chickens *en route* to roost.

The Board's anxiety was easy to understand. They said they recognised, perhaps only now, that the process was leading to the most significant structural shift in our history. They recognised their own responsibility to ensure the organisation gets it right. Not having been adequately connected, they didn't feel sure. Dr Joe Remenyi, a Deakin University development academic who had been on the Board for five years, broke the quiet that followed.

"It looks like it comes down to whether or not we trust Philip."

Exactly. There was just enough silence for that brick in my stomach to turn into despair. The Board usually worked toward a consensus. I hoped this time for a vote. Vainly.

"I do not believe I should be made a scapegoat for the Board's inadequate process," I said, my political skills having deserted me. "If I do not have your trust, you can have my resignation." I did not mean it as a challenge. It was a matter of fact.

At least that prompted a response. "It's not come to that," from Professor Breward in the chair. "We just need to find the way to bring the Board back into the process."

"A small committee," I forget who proposed it. "Three or four Board members to work with Philip on issues and modifications to the process." OK? That didn't sound too bad. So, we could continue? Yes. The Board appointed Peter King, Bruce Redpath, Simon McKeon and Anita Wynne to my new steering committee. I agreed and thanked the Board.

But the fun was not yet over. We proceeded to an election for the new chair. I knew already that there were two candidates, Peter King and Simon McKeon. They had each been approached and agreed to stand. They represented fresh blood with not a lot of World Vision history.

Peter had the advantage of his international involvement with David in the Partnership Review, but neither had spent time at the sharp end of World Vision. Simon was a future *Australian of the Year*. A successful money man with the millionaires factory, Macquarie Bank. His attendance at meetings always interrupted by mobile calls on the current million-dollar deal. Of the two, I preferred Simon. He was easy-going and nearer my age. I did not know how I would find him as a chair.

We got a new chair (I understood later by a single vote) and it was Peter King. There were lovely words said and minuted about David Jenkin and his contribution, which I heartily endorsed.

I shook Peter's hand in congratulations. Reminded him I was flying out in the morning to the international meetings and we agreed to meet immediately on my return.

"We'll get this committee moving," Peter said encouragingly.

"Great," I responded hopefully.

* * *

55

Talk To Peers—You Are Not On This Journey Alone

From the Howard Johnson's hotel in Monrovia, Los Angeles, I sent a fax to Peter. I had asked my colleague, Tina Fairlie, to see if she could get the new Board Committee together. Apparently, it was called the Organisational Restructuring Working Group, which seemed a mouthful not of my penmanship. I would be back on Saturday, 2nd September. Perhaps we could get everyone together on the Monday.

In the meantime, I asked Tina to send the members a complete set of the various reports, which by now compiled into a tome. Perhaps, on reading, they would have more confidence in the trajectory the staff had produced.

Two blocks further East on Route 66 from my hotel, the senior leadership of World Vision was meeting in the Partnership Team. The three largest support offices, USA, Canada and Australia, talked about organisational change. Don Scott, President of World Vision Canada, reported they were "re-engineering".

"It's hard," Don admitted. "It's really important how it's led. The consultants we hired just don't seem to understand us." It worried him that the mood was becoming negative.

Bob Seiple, President of World Vision US, also had his worries. He wanted to move the entire office two thousand kilometres from Los Angeles to Seattle. It made our little shift from South Melbourne to Burwood East look like a Sunday drive.

"It's going remarkably well," said Bob, "but it creates enormous stress. People react in unexpected ways. And some people are physically sick. It might be related."

His Board had split 11-7 in favour of the move. It worried Bob.

"When you're fully on the offensive," Bob said, "and you've got the whole staff moving with you, you don't want the Board looking over your shoulder."

I felt much less alone for a few days. Even as I published a *Trellis* to the staff at home communicating these things we had in common with the women and men in North America, I was expecting to pick up the momentum with my new Organisational Restructuring Working Group.

* * *

56

Cut Off At The Pass

Peter King and Tina had negotiated a meeting of the ORWG for the following Wednesday. We would meet in Simon McKeon's office in the city.

Early in the process, I had invited Rod Wakefield to leave behind his job as World Vision's Queensland State Manager to occupy an office near mine and help me guide the process. It had been an inspired choice. Rod quickly understood what I was attempting and made it possible for me to keep working as the CEO, even while we attempted an organisational revolution.

World Vision couldn't stop dead while we rearranged our furniture. All the usual work—finding supporters, caring for them—all had to go ahead. We were on parallel paths and Rod could concentrate fully on the new track. Naturally, we also had to prepare the operating plan for 1996 and get it through the Board. There, our CFO Boyne Alley, who just did everything needed without fuss or complaint, ably supported me. Nevertheless, we felt stretched. Now we had a Board working group added to the mix. It was easy to feel that something might give.

Simon's city office was way up in the air with a view across South Melbourne towards Port Phillip Bay. You could see our old building down there. It had become an apartment tower. Simon guided Rod and me into a meeting room where Peter was already waiting. My expectation was that we had come to a working meeting of this new group. Two of the members were not present. I was about to ask if we should wait for them, but Peter spoke.

"The Board's position is that we need to put a pause on the change process," he said, matter of fact.

"A pause? What does that mean?" I asked. It was obvious the Board needed to catch up, but I still clung to a fading hope that we could keep the momentum going with the staff.

"Well, just put things on hold. For the time being."

I was not ready for this. Rod and I had come prepared to go through the reports and papers the staff process had generated. We thought this would be a meeting of the working group. We came to work. Maybe I said something like that, but Peter was clear.

"A pause," he repeated. "I have access to a good consultant in organisational change." A little devil in my head was saying *Tell him he already has a CEO who is good in organisational change.* "I need to see when he could come and work with the Board and the senior staff."

I was on a fast learning curve of how Peter's chairmanship would be less strategic and more managerial than his predecessor. Also, that ideas like "the Board's position" might rely on the intuition of the chair.

The meeting went nowhere after this. Simon chipped in with encouragement, but the noise in my head drowned out his cheeriness. How was I going to tell the team back at 1 Vision Drive? We had built up such a perfect wave. We could feel the push on our hips as we looked down the arc of rushing water. We were ready to thrill with the impetus of all our pre-work adding momentum towards the golden beach. On such a full sea we were now afloat.

Or were we soon to lose our ventures and be bound in shallows and miseries?

I could do nothing but agree. I would have to find a workaround. Keep the herd heading west, while these outliers could be nudged back in. I was not at all confident, but I would try.

And, anyway, I had a supporter dinner to host in a few minutes at the MCG. Life demanded a cool head and a steady voice.

James Mageria, VP Africa, had been in town all week. Tonight was the highlight of the week as we introduced him to a full house of supporters. I was the host. I needed to detach myself from that last hour and be host to these precious people who loved our work enough to send us their money. Somehow, perhaps on induced adrenalin, the night seemed to go very well.

Later, Rod said, "I don't know how you did that. After that meeting with Peter and Simon ... well, you were such a good compere." His affirmation touched me. With colleagues like this, one felt anything was achievable.

What about the ORWG, the Board-appointed Organisational Restructuring Working Group? If it ever met, I never saw any evidence. Perhaps they met under Chatham House rules. Or perhaps our new chair preferred just one hand on the tiller.

* * *

57

The End Of One Story

It was the end of the story as far as organisational change at World Vision Australia. At least while I remained their CEO.

Over the next months a few colleagues worked on next steps in hope, but in early November I met Peter's chosen consultant. Adrian Dart was a competent guy with a competent process. He began by circulating 13 questions for each of the attendees. They were good questions; I wanted him to get a sense of the diversity of ideas in our Board/Senior Staff group. I put my name on top, but I noted it was optional. I wondered if anyone might not want to own up to their answers. Surely not?

A first workshop with the Board alone (me present) confirmed how far apart we were. It felt like *my desk* syndrome; as if they could not see beyond what was right in front of them. The newer members, especially, could not see our Australian entity as part of a larger, more diverse, whole. Some of them seemed unable to see beyond a single fundraising program—*Child Sponsorship*. I regretted my failure to push the Board for a more comprehensive orientation for new members. I had not seen it as my responsibility. And maybe it wasn't, but a better CEO wouldn't have been so reluctant to intervene.

A month later, the Board met with our senior team. How would this go? It was awful. So much pain and anger in the room. There was a Gestalt, stuff under the table, that Adrian's process could never address. It was a fiasco. I felt sorry for our facilitator, but it was not surprising.

There was value in Adrian's approach. Ideas around "mission" or "intent" bounced around all morning. Finally, they settled on something quite refreshing. A "worldwide" mission statement: "New Hope for All" sub-texted by an Australian mission statement: "Every Aussie a Helper". I wondered if we might draw together. I ached for what we might have achieved if we had done this a year earlier. It is what I had wanted but felt powerless to make happen. Did it really require a change in Board leadership?

After lunch, Adrian asked, "What's really in our heart?" I loved that he was already including himself, even while I recognised it as a tactic. "But you can't have six."

But we did have six. Our Core Values. The whole of World Vision had worked at the end of the previous decade developing them. These statements had become part of the furniture. I had never challenged them. I felt they were still right. Yet, I liked what Adrian was doing. Had we really thought about this? Adrian was boldly suggesting "you can only have two!" It sounded heretical. Yet it might have had a touch of Luther about it.

The challenge hung in the air.

Later, as Adrian and I walked by our main conference room, we passed the six wall panels proclaiming the Six Core Values.

He smiled. "Are you going to take four of them down?" I chuckled.

Next was a discussion about *DRIVING FORCES*. I imagined Adrian spoke his labels capitalised. Maybe it was the effect of his South African accent.

Then, *MARKETS*. Which markets do we serve? This came out in a familiar place—individuals, groups, governments.

Aware of our staff attempts to match markets with products, Adrian led us through a first cut on developing a market/product structure. *Déjà vu* for staff and no coherent answer for all the bits that seemed left out. I guessed Adrian was showing us a method if we wanted to use it. He was illustrating, not prescribing. We rushed through CAPABILITY DEVELOPMENT, then GROWTH/PROFIT to ACTION PLANS.

Two Board members agreed to firm up the Intent Statement, and the Core Values discussion. The Management Team were asked to develop the market/product matrix, performance guidelines, and growth goals.

Towards the end of the day, I tried to be more and more silent. Changing the organisation was terrifying me. Letting the group wisdom play itself out was taking enormous self-discipline. My desire to offer my own wisdom had me knotted up. Yet, if I did this, I stole discovery from the group. And only discovery would lead to commitment.

The process contrasted with the earlier Future Search method. Adrian's system was more familiar to me than Future Search. It had an MBA feeling about it. This process was validating the role of the Board and that could hardly be a bad thing. Future Search had validated the staff. Both processes were disempowering the management team. Certainly they believed so. I had tried to compensate by ensuring the management team members were leaders in the steps that followed.

The Board's interest in rethinking our vision, mission and intent completely broadsided me. I remained fully committed to our earlier work. We were *fighting poverty by empowering people to transform their worlds*. We did not need to review it. We needed to make it real, to live it.

Around the middle of the day, I allowed myself to think, "What if the Board is right? What if we need to change our strategic vision?" That's when I realised it would mean all our planning would have to stop. Our planning had affirmed our vision as fixed, sorted, resolved. We had dealt with the question of strategic intent first—in the Future Search process. If the Board wanted to debate strategic vision, they too, must do that first.

Over the Christmas-New Year period, I suggested a process that the Board might meet with the management team in retreat. There already was a booking at Jumbunna Lodge, in the hills East of Melbourne. I waited in vain to get a response.

Since the *pause*, morale had fallen. Coincidentally, we had scheduled a routine annual survey of corporate culture for late September. The psychologist reported:

> The effect on morale has been palpable. Volunteers reported a clear change in organisational mood. The survey of 200 staff members revealed 57% with moderate or significant fatigue, 59% anxious or worried, 48% pessimistic, 40% angry or irritable, 50% feeling isolated, 43% feeling distrustful or suspicious, and 45% with self-doubts. Sixty-one percent of staff felt that productivity levels were lower than before. These feelings increased by 25% after the "pause".

But what to do? If the Board wanted business-as-usual, or even business-according-to-some-other-way, I still had the responsibility. The Board approved the 1996 Operating Plan, and we got to work. I pulled Peter King and another Board member into that retreat with the management team in the New Year, which proved helpful in establishing an effective relationship within the expanded group.

There was one glimmer of light. I invited the young Tim Costello to the retreat for a session. He met with us over lunch and then shared for two hours. Eight years later, the Board invited him to lead World Vision Australia.

Staff wanted to know how things were under the new Chair. I replied honestly that Peter and I were beginning to understand each other's needs. I realised he wanted more information. He was a manager at heart, and he wanted more detail than David. I would tell people I thought we had got things "back on the rails" even though, privately, I no longer knew where these rails were leading.

In June, I announced that we were focussed on producing a "balanced scorecard". This is what the Board had voted for, and I gave it the best spin I could. But my heart was heavy. I felt I was telling my colleagues less than the truth. I made no mention of transformation. It was illusory to think I could revive our revolution, and I did not try. That wave had gone. Our job was to manage in the shallows.

I did wonder in darker moments whether my failure to make change stick was just as simple as I thought—the consequence of a new Board majority, holding naïve understandings of the organisation, combined with a new take-charge chair. Maybe not that simple.

Perhaps rather, it was a brilliant strategy. Peter King did want to take charge of organisational direction. Could Peter King have been clever enough to see that he could not slow the momentum of change by attacking our work of the past year? He would need to target something we had accepted without question—the organisation's vision, values and intent.

But I don't think such a view is fair to Peter, or the Board. Undoubtedly, Peter took his responsibilities seriously and he acted as his background in commercial business equipped. He brought a vision of what World Vision was that was different from mine. We each thought the other wrong. He had a job to do, and he would need to do it the way he understood it. I was the same. The two were, regrettably, not reconcilable.

Regardless, my dream of organisational change at 1 Vision Drive was evaporating through lack of nurture. The engine of change idled into silence.

* * *

58

Drifting

Despite disappointment, I wasn't sad. I know that probably sounds strange. I had pinned my colours to a change process that was derailed. True. I felt the setback, but World Vision was a big place. It was not like I had nothing to do. And what I had to do brought satisfaction and, quite often, real joy.

The New Year saw the family on annual leave in Marysville again. The birds eat out of your hand at Blackwood Cottages. And seven-year-old boys and their Mum and Dad play cricket on the Marysville oval. Mum shows Rich how it is possible to bowl with your right arm and bat with your left. He learns the word *ambidextrous* with which he will impress his Grade 2 teacher in a few weeks.

An innovation appeared in 1996—The Peer Review Process. An international team would review each World Vision entity over a 3-5-year period. New Zealand and the U.K. were on my list for a week in January and September, respectively. The freshly minted director of Peer Reviews, Alastair Greaves, appointed me to a 5-person bunch of peers for my trip across the Tasman. Later in the year I chaired the Review Team in the UK. It was an encouraging experience based on the idea of alignment around shared values. It held promise for a more effective World Vision partnership.

Back at the office, I admit I felt rudderless. 1995 had been so excitingly hard. Now, with the spark of change practically extinguished, it was back to normal. But normal was boring. I enrolled in a Doctor of Management program at RMIT, which I found immediately stimulating. I finished the final edit of a book, *Journeys to Justice*. Harper Collins soon published it. A little publicity accrued World Vision's way. The book satisfied me, although Glenda Orland, who later became a novelist herself, reviewed it accurately with the comment "I was confused whether I was reading a novel or a textbook."

I went to the usual international meetings and played my part. In May I was invited to a "Gyngell Meeting". Bruce Gyngell had been helping World Vision Australia voluntarily for about a decade. Famous as "the first face on Australian television" in 1956, Bruce had many firsts. First head of SBS. First head of the Australian Broadcasting Tribunal. Head of both the Seven and Nine networks at different times. The inspiration behind *Bandstand* in the 1960s, for which I was grateful. Head of TV-AM and Yorkshire Television in Britain. And personal advisor to a series of World Vision Communications executives after me.

The *Gyngell Meeting* owed something to Dave Toycen and Warwick Olson (from Pilgrim, our Ad Agency). It involved a meeting with Bruce at whatever place he was taking a holiday with his family. It happened about once a year and Bruce, who you might guess couldn't stop working, would give over two days reviewing all of World Vision Australia's television programming and advertising. For free.

I wasn't part of this annual *fabularama* except in 1996. John Rose should get the credit for inviting me, although he does remind me that I hinted. Maybe he felt sorry for me and, generous as usual, knew I would enjoy the gig.

This year the venue was Hilton Head, South Carolina, about 2 hours' drive from Charleston where my daughter's family would live twenty years later while our son-in-law built Boeing 787s. It was relaxing and reinvigorating. I'd met Bruce a few times. He'd dined me and Warwick Olson at his Club in London once, where I foolishly offered to pay for the wine. The bottle was so expensive I decided against claiming it on travel expenses. At Hilton Head it was a privilege to see the deep knowledge of this legendary figure being laid out for World Vision as a gift. If you asked Bruce why, which I did once, he replied, "Your people impressed me. They were honest, godly people. I enjoyed being with them."

I am telling you this story because of what happened on the last day in Hilton Head. Dean Hirsch, who had succeeded Graeme Irvine as President of World Vision International, took me aside.

"I'm thinking of bringing Bruce McConchie into the international office as a chief operating officer," Dean said. "I'd value your opinion."

My opinion was wholeheartedly positive. Bruce would be a splendid choice. After outstanding work at World Vision New Zealand, Bruce had become a fixer. Right now, he was sorting out the Middle East and Eastern Europe operations—the newest and smallest of World Vision's regions after Asia, Africa and Latin America.

"Who will you replace Bruce with?" I asked.

"Your name has been mentioned."

I uttered a single HA! in surprise. "Why?"

Dean explained that my role in advocacy on the Palestine question had been obvious. I appeared to have an interest there. He was right, but North and East of the Mediterranean were hardly my strong suits.

"And I thought you might be ready for a fresh challenge."

"Well, I have that already, Dean," I said. "Last year was disappointing but that's history now. I needed to change the way I relate to the Board, especially Peter, and I think we're OK. Anyway, Judy and I have already had our overseas experience in Hong Kong. I don't think she wants another one. You need to presume the answer is 'No'. Thanks, but no thanks."

I gave the matter no further thought. My work was at home. There was unfinished work. I was less confident that I could right the ship, but I did not for a second consider abandonment.

Conversations after re-immersion into family life tended to be episodic, sandwiched between unpacking, putting out the laundry, have a coffee, watching some telly, and pillow talk. Over the next day or two I gradually told Judy about the meetings, about the beauty of

South Carolina, that *shagging* meant a different thing in that part of the world, about the Gyngell family, and about the new job offers Dean was making to staff.

"You know," Judy said, "if Dean ever offered you a job in somewhere nice like Geneva. That'd be alright."

Now, this woman I'd married liked a predictable life. She liked routine and sometimes suggested she was a wimp, but she was a brave wimp. The future might always look dangerous but if she had her family around her, she knew she would cope. Our experience as a family in Hong Kong had taught Judy that she was capable of much more than she'd imagined.

"Sit down, dear" I said, and came clean on the job offer.

"Sounds good. You could do that," Judy assured me.

And then the question that mattered more than whether her husband could do the job. "Where would we live?"

"Vienna."

"That'd be nice, wouldn't it?"

I started as Vice-President for the Middle East and Eastern Europe on 2nd January 1997. The last six months at World Vision Australia was time for tying up loose ends, keeping the ship sailing straight, and brushing up on our German.

There was one final *contretemps* with Peter King. It involved the Prime Minister, John Howard.

On 29th October 1996, the member for Oxley, the egregious Pauline Hanson, rose to ask a question:

"My question is directed to the Prime Minister. I believe, along with millions of other Australians, that as the leader of Australia your first and main obligation is to the people of Australia. Would you consider reducing our foreign aid, which runs at approximately $1.5 billion a year, to create a civil national service for our youth, to enable them and others to gain employment, as well as personal and social gains, through the building of roads, bridges, railway lines, reafforestation and water conservation systems, to name a few national projects?"

Hanson built a reputation on fallacious comparisons. If I had been offering an answer, I would have pointed this out. John Howard, with a nod to Hanson's right-wing base, trod his own path.

After politely thanking Ms Hanson for her question, Mr Howard continued:

"It is equally true that on occasions Australians legitimately feel that foreign aid is sometimes not as effectively used as it might be. I can understand the anger in that. I can understand the anger of Australians who give money voluntarily to great organisations like World Vision and so forth, seeing the political perfidy of regimes in different parts of the world which allows that aid to be literally wasted on the wharves, airports and railway sidings of countries whose citizens are suffering appalling deprivation."

Within minutes a transcript appeared in my emails. Appalling. I pulled out the essence of his third sentence. "Australians…give money …to…World Vision…and (then)…the regimes…allow that aid to be literally wasted." Sorry, Mr Howard. That is a lie. On so many levels.

First, World Vision's business model was to work local. We hardly ever shipped aid in from other countries because we could nearly always get it locally. Second, we used our own systems to secure, transport and deliver aid. We didn't involve governments. And we never, ever, handed World Vision emergency relief over to governments to distribute. Everyone knew that was a recipe for theft and corruption.

I had witnessed the diligence with which we tracked emergency aid end-to-end.

In Somalia I had watched another agency drive to a village and throw bags of grain off the back of the truck. That meant the strongmen of the village took control. That agency turned a gift into a profitable business for the strongmen.

This was not World Vision's way. We ensured there was organisation. No food riots, no theft, local involvement under watchful eyes.

Our media team issued a press release pointing out that Mr Howard had lied about World Vision and asked him to correct the record. ABC News thought it was interesting enough to get me to say so on camera.

Peter King, who I suspected to be a member of the Liberal Party, was apoplectic.

"You can't call the Prime Minister a liar" he infuriated down the telephone. There was not a lot of upside in having an argument. "You can't do that," Peter blustered.

I so wanted to say, *Well I can, and I just did.* Instead, I said, "Well, what the PM said about World Vision was wrong. We don't allow aid to rot on wharves. We don't pass our aid onto governments."

"But you went on the news!"

"Yes." I thought that a splendid thing. I was often on the news. Name recognition, mate.

"They will be offended," advised Peter.

"Who?" *They*? Who are *they*?

"The Government. They won't appreciate us criticising them."

There was more of this. An implication that the millions in aid that we delivered for the Government might somehow be in jeopardy. Could the PM be so thin-skinned? I doubted it completely.

I got out of the conversation without agreeing to a retraction. The Sydney Morning Herald and The Age reported my comments the next morning. John Howard wrapped up the matter with a politically clever statement.

"In this morning's edition of the *Sydney Morning Herald*, Mr Michael Seccombe, from the gallery, makes the claim in his column that I had said yesterday in answer to a question from the member for Oxley (Ms Hanson) that a lot of money—both that given by the Government and that given through organisations like World Vision—was wasted. The clear inference is that I was suggesting that giving money to World Vision was a waste. I did not say that, nor did I infer it. What I did say and infer was that I could understand the anger of people who gave money to great organisations like World Vision, seeing the political perfidy of regimes in different parts of the world which allows that aid to be literally wasted on the wharves, airports and railways.

"The truth of the matter is that the wasting is a direct result of the behaviour of regimes and not that of organisations like World Vision, which are outstanding humanitarian organisations."

The response was an example of Howard's political skill. He claimed to not "infer". Strictly, he should have said "I did not mean to *imply*" since an inference is something that only a hearer can draw. But that is exactly what he hoped the listeners, especially those who supported Ms Hanson, would infer. Namely, that aid of any kind, Government or World Vision, was a waste. A mid-90s example of what later we called *dog-whistling*.

As I was writing this book, I had lunch with Tim Costello, who had become my favourite World Vision Australia CEO for giving the organisation such a powerful voice. Tim's memoir, *A Lot with A Little*, was just hitting the bookstores. I found resonance in the events on pages 213 and 214. I noted that between my leaving and Tim's arriving the Board had revoked the longstanding authority of the CEO to be the spokesperson. This was an authority that Tim bravely assumed, put it to the test, and regained.

My final shot across the bows appeared in the annual financial statements. My outraged heart was evidenced on my sleeve.

* * *

Copy for Annual Financial Report

It is time for a reality check. Much is said about the accountability of charitable bodies like World Vision Australia. This is a good thing. This annual report is one way that World Vision provides accountability to supporters and other interested people.

But it's time for a little perspective.

During this past year, a Government-sponsored investigation reported positively on the effectiveness of organisations such as World Vision. This followed the previous year's investigation by the Industry Commission into Charitable Institutions, one of the commission's most expensive ever. It demonstrated that charitable groups are the least in need of being investigated.

Nevertheless, Government and the public (usually not supporters themselves) have increased demands for audits and double and triple checks. These add administrative inefficiencies to already efficient systems. We comply because we must. And to refuse to comply allows people to draw the wrong conclusion that we do not care about accountability.

But enough is enough. Much of this looks like diversionary tactics. Attack the charitable sector because it is an easy mark. Meanwhile extraordinary incompetence goes unnoticed, unreported and unfixed in government and business.

Two issues are worth noting in particular. First, that the Australian Government's official aid program (paid out of our taxes) is now of low quality and dubious benefit to the poor. Second, that the Australian Government is failing in its responsibility to tackle global poverty in a meaningful way. Its only saving grace is that few other governments are doing any better.

I am sure most World Vision supporters think that our Government aid, like our gifts through World Vision, is being used mostly to help poor people. Sorry to say, it is not the case. And in some cases where the intent is to meet basic human needs, the funds are allocated through the UN system when Australian agencies like World Vision with a track record of effectiveness can deliver the aid more efficiently.

The second issue is that perhaps for the first time in history the world has the know-how, the ability and the resources to conquer world poverty. It simply requires the political will to fund the right programs. The global bill to eliminate poverty is around $340 billion a year. Or less than a third of what the world presently spends on armaments.

Admittedly much of the distorted spending priorities are in the very Third World countries where a real poverty focus is required, but leadership ought to be coming from the rich nations who have the resources to invest. And the democratic processes to hold their elected representatives accountable.

Instead, the world is turning its back on this opportunity. No logic can justify such opportunistic stupidity or such breathtaking short-sightedness.

Looking back over this last year at World Vision Australia I am delighted that there are many thousands of Australians who have greater vision, and greater commitment to the future we are creating for our children. Public support for World Vision has grown during this last year, while Government investment in the poor through World Vision is in serious decline.

So, we are not at all discouraged. Thanks to you, and the many thousands like you, we see that there is a vision for a better world in this country. That people care and will invest in programs that are seriously and effectively tackling poverty. That we are getting the job done, even if the world is not yet getting enough of it done.

Thank you for being a partner with World Vision in providing answers to the needs of the world. We look forward to the day when your example and leadership is rewarded by a world in which poverty is banished to history. And that's for real!

Blessings, Philip

* * *

59

Afterword

Leaving World Vision Australia was not the end of my leadership life. Instead, it represented a transition. Out of the sorrows came a time for re-assessment. Was I any good at this game?

The Peter Principle, named after its author, Laurence J. Peter, states that *People rise to their level of incompetence*. I wondered if that described me. Had I over-reached *my* competence? Had I tried to do more than I could deliver? My confidence had taken a shaking, but I had time during 1996 to review what had happened. With hindsight, I could see I would have done some things differently, but that is the dubious benefit of hindsight. It is not a ruler by which to measure competence in real time.

I believed there were countless organisations in which I could work, plan, improve, encourage, and lead. When I was a radio DJ in Brisbane, I had never thought I could be useful in marketing and fundraising for an overseas aid organisation. When I was Communications Director for World Vision Australia it never occurred to me that my skills might be useful in setting up a World Vision entity in Hong Kong. I became certain there were new adventures in leadership somewhere. I admit, I did not expect them to start in Vienna.

We spent four years in Austria. As VP for Middle East and Eastern Europe, I had about a thousand staff stretching from Russia to Palestine. We operated out of a small office, two floors up from World Vision Österreich, the local fundraising office. Vienna was the only place one could get flights to everywhere one needed to go. Later, Cyprus became more suitable.

We lived, Austrian-style, in a 2-bedroom apartment in the 18th District of Vienna. Richard, now nearly nine, went to the American International School, just up the road. I spent many weeks visiting the dozen field offices, but nearly always I was home for the weekends. We took holidays in unforgettable parts of Austria. We visited relatives in France. Our older kids, Jamie and Melanie, visited and once Jamie saw the snow, he stayed in Europe for years.

Concentrating on developing the leadership team throughout the region and Board development in Romania, we built a good team who grew the work and responded to times of rapid change. We worked alongside the remnants of the disintegration of the Soviet bloc and Yugoslavia. I was glad to say we kept World Vision work on a good trajectory.

After four years, we came back to Oz so that Richard, now entering High School, could be in his own country and culture. This was a conscious family commitment, and it meant my 24-year journey with World Vision was over.

Back in our Boronia home I went to work in the management consulting world. I yearned for something less sporadic; Judy yearned for less sporadic income.

An interesting assignment presented itself at Deakin University. The Vice-Chancellor, in a last act before departure, had required more than a dozen separate student associations to become just one. I took on the job as General Manager of the newly minted Deakin University Student Association (DUSA) and stayed five years. This was fascinating, fun and hard work, although a daughter of one former colleague wondered, "He's doing what? Is that like a hobby?"

It was no hobby and not improved by John Howard when, in cahoots with Peter Costello, the Government forced the universities to cut off funding. Since DUSA had several businesses on campus, we were not bereft. But when the government removes $5 million from a $15 million turnover, circumstance requires change-management skills.

In 2008, I made my own position redundant at DUSA and began a similar turnaround job at Foodbank. Also, the result of a shotgun wedding, Dame Phyllis Frost's ancient organisation, VicRelief, and the more modern, Foodbank, merged. Funded by the Victorian Department of Human Services, they decided that only a merged organisation would get the money.

In time, the organisation became known as Foodbank Victoria, like its mates in other States. I had the pleasure of setting it on a steady keel in a little over two years, and appointing Dave McNamara. Dave later became CEO and has guided the organisation to its status as the major supplier of food to the charities of Victoria, and a household name.

Working at Deakin had frequently taken us to Warrnambool where Deakin had a campus, and our dream of retirement in Marysville moved five hours South-West. In 2010 we sold our Boronia house of 30 years and moved to the Coast where we could "see Tasmania from the kitchen window." Allegedly.

We settled into the retired life. We found friends and faith at the Warrnambool Presbyterian Church and they had a pipe organ out of which I helped blow the dust. I helped manage the church in a two-million-dollar project that resulted in a new multi-purpose hall beside the heritage 1880s church.

In late 2018, I saw that Rob Buckingham, senior minister of a Pentecostal Church in Cheltenham, Melbourne, was looking for a General Manager. I'd known Rob from my time on the Board of *Light FM*, where Rob had been the part-time Music Director. I often read his blog and enjoyed his reflections. So, for a time, we rented our Warrnambool home unit and relocated to Mordialloc. I returned to work for an interesting and stimulating two years.

As I shifted offices from one organisation to the next, I found many things that were familiar—stuff I already knew. And also, many things that were sufficiently similar for me to be able to adapt what I knew to new environments. There was less learning to lead in this phase of my work, and more learning to apply what I knew.

Maybe that's another story about leadership. Perhaps I should write it.

* * *

About The Author

After many years of radio, communications and managerial leadership experience (as described in this book), Philip and his wife Judith have settled back at the western end of Victoria's Great Ocean Road, Warrnambool, Australia. They have three adult children and six grandchildren.

Philip loves to read, write, and cycle. He also plays the piano every day.

You can enjoy more of Philip's writing and many talents on his personal website:

https://philiphunt.com

Cardinia Ranges Publishing House is an Australian publisher with the mission:

Inspiring people to fulfill their God-given potential

Works are published under the following imprints:

Cardinia Ranges Publishing House
General trade fiction and non-fiction works of encouragement, inspiration and personal development

—

Cardinia Ranges Education
Curriculum and teaching resources that challenge and inspire

—

CRYA
Young Adult fiction works that thrill, engage and inspire

—

Little Cockatoos
Children's picture and story books that inspire

—

Gold-Crested Press
A quality imprint for self-publishing authors

For more information:

Visit the website: cardiniaranges.com
Or follow on social media: CardiniaRanges

Share your thoughts on this work and leave a review via
cardiniaranges.com/books/review

www.ingramcontent.com/pod-product-compliance
Lightning Source LLC
Chambersburg PA
CBHW021140080526
44588CB00008B/140